Praise for *What's the Worst That Could Happen?*

"Greg Craven has written a brilliant and unique work on global warming. His innovative and intelligent approach to this controversial issue is superbly crafted. It is an important book that is a must-read for those who care about our planet and future generations."

—General Anthony C. Zinni, USMC (Retired)

"This book trumps most of our accounts of the global warming crisis, partly for its good humor and straightforward logic, and partly because the author has actually figured out what actions make sense. Changing your lightbulb will help a little, but changing the political debate will help enormously—and this book will get you started down that path."

—Bill McKibben, author of *The End of Nature*

"The worst thing that could happen is that you don't read this book! Greg Craven has written a valuable primer on the global warming debate."

—Gregg Easterbrook, author of *Sonic Boom*

"This is a tremendous book and well worth anyone's time to read. It very clearly and concisely covers all of the important points not only about the climate change situation in our moment, but also how we think and decide about important issues. Anyone who enjoyed Craven's YouTube triumph 'The Most Terrifying Video You'll Ever See' will enjoy unpacking that experience in this book, and for people running into Craven for the first time, you're in for a treat—he is funny as well as exceptionally clear and wise."

—Kim Stanley Robinson, the Hugo and Nebula Award–winning author of the Mars trilogy and *Science in the Capital*

What's the Worst That Could Happen?

A RATIONAL RESPONSE TO THE CLIMATE CHANGE DEBATE

Greg Craven

A Perigee Book

A PERIGEE BOOK
Published by the Penguin Group
Penguin Group (USA) Inc.
375 Hudson Street, New York, New York 10014, USA
Penguin Group (Canada), 90 Eglinton Avenue East, Suite 700, Toronto, Ontario M4P 2Y3, Canada
(a division of Pearson Penguin Canada Inc.)
Penguin Books Ltd., 80 Strand, London WC2R 0RL, England
Penguin Group Ireland, 25 St. Stephen's Green, Dublin 2, Ireland (a division of Penguin Books Ltd.)
Penguin Group (Australia), 250 Camberwell Road, Camberwell, Victoria 3124, Australia
(a division of Pearson Australia Group Pty. Ltd.)
Penguin Books India Pvt. Ltd., 11 Community Centre, Panchsheel Park, New Delhi—110 017, India
Penguin Group (NZ), 67 Apollo Drive, Rosedale, North Shore 0632, New Zealand
(a division of Pearson New Zealand Ltd.)
Penguin Books (South Africa) (Pty.) Ltd., 24 Sturdee Avenue, Rosebank, Johannesburg 2196,
South Africa

Penguin Books Ltd., Registered Offices: 80 Strand, London WC2R 0RL, England

While the author has made every effort to provide accurate telephone numbers and Internet addresses at the time of publication, neither the publisher nor the author assumes any responsibility for errors, or for changes that occur after publication. Further, the publisher does not have any control over and does not assume any responsibility for author or third-party websites or their content.

First edition: July 2009

Library of Congress Cataloging-in-Publication Data

Craven, Greg.
  What's the worst that could happen? : a rational response to the climate change debate / Greg Craven.— 1st ed.
      p.   cm.
  Includes bibliographical references and index.
  ISBN 978-0-399-53501-7
  1. Climatic changes.   2. Global warming.   I. Title
  QC981.8.C5C7665 2009
  363.738'74—dc22   2009005375

PRINTED IN THE UNITED STATES OF AMERICA

10 9 8 7 6 5 4 3 2 1

Most Perigee books are available at special quantity discounts for bulk purchases for sales promotions, premiums, fund-raising, or educational use. Special books, or book excerpts, can also be created to fit specific needs. For details, write: Special Markets, Penguin Group (USA) Inc., 375 Hudson Street, New York, New York 10014.

CONTENTS

This is for Katie and Alex.

SHOULD I BOTHER TO READ THIS BOOK?

Are you as sick of all the shouting about global warming as I am? On the one hand, you have the entire U.S. intelligence community issuing a report that says global warming is a national security issue that should be taken seriously—ASAP. On the other, you have a senior senator calling global warming "the greatest hoax ever perpetuated by the American people," and he's got a list of 400 scientists who agree with him. You're not ready to dismiss the possibility that your own security may be threatened, but you've got limited time, and you're put off by the sheer amount of arguments ricocheting around like bullets.

What is the harried lay person supposed to do? If you're like most people, you probably feel as if you were under assault. And you're skeptical of swallowing what people tell you because you suspect they're just trying to manipulate you to serve their own interests. (Including me!) So, rather than step into the mess yourself to decide who's right, you're inclined to just let the two sides have at each other while you wait for the dust to clear. That's generally worked out in the past.

But can it work this time? According to the global warming activists, there is a big timer ticking away while we debate, and if we let it run down, we won't just get some weenie little buzzer, but a 100,000-volt charge across the floor, audience included.

That doesn't mean they're right. But it does sort of raise the sense of urgency for the casual observer, doesn't it? The activists argue that if we do not make a decision for ourselves very soon, then the laws of physics will decide for us. Although we are trying to avoid making an unwise decision by waiting

THE ACTIVISTS SHRIEK

The globe is warming!

We're the ones doing it!

It's gonna be a catastrophe!

Panic! The wolf is at the door!

This is the biggest threat in human history!

Waiting any longer would be too expensive!

There is nothing more worth spending our money on than this!

If we don't take drastic action, the climate and everything in it is *doomed*!

We've got to act now, now, *now*!

The science *is* settled!

Science doesn't operate by petition!

You're biased!

You're just a greedy libertarian corporate shill, looking after your own selfish gain!

You've fought this so hard that the credibility of conservatives and libertarians is now completely on the line! You guys are going to be so totally hosed when you turn out to be wrong. No one will listen to you ever again!

In 20 years, when the carbon hits the fan, you are all going to be lined up against the wall for dragging the rest of us down with your shortsighted selfishness!

Ahhhh! Look! Look! It's already happening! Cut carbon emissions to zero *now*! Mitigate! Mitigate!

THE SKEPTICS APPEASE

- The globe is not warming.
- It's a natural cycle.
- It'll be harmless.
- Chill out. The wolf is not at the door.
- No, this is the biggest hoax in history.
- Taking big action would be too expensive.
- There are a ton of things more worth spending our money on than this.
- If we do take drastic action, the economy and everything in it is *doomed*!
- Let's wait until the science is settled.
- I've got a petition right here that says it isn't.
- Science doesn't operate by authority!
- No, you're biased!
- You're just an enviroweenie Chicken Little, looking to control people and start a New World Order!
- You've screeched a false alarm so loudly that the credibility of science itself is on the line! You guys are going to be so totally hosed when you turn out to be wrong. No one will trust the scientific establishment for 100 years.
- In 20 years, when your hysterical groupthink and conspiracy are revealed for all to see, you are all going to be lined up against the wall for your corrupt ploy to get money and control!
- It's too big to do anything about! Cutting emissions would throw us back to the dark ages! Keep the economy strong so we can deal with this! Adapt! Adapt!

until the issue is settled, in a sense we are constantly making a decision by default: the decision to not take big action yet. Perhaps that is the best decision. But I, for one, want that choice to be a deliberate one.

As a high school science teacher for 9 years, my job has been to translate science for people who don't necessarily care for the stuff. So maybe I can help you untangle the climate change snarl and take the decision-making process back into your own hands rather than leaving it to the whims of fate.

Here's the good news: I'm *not* going to do that by offering up yet another hair ball of graphs and footnotes to convince you which side is right. There are plenty of other books out there on both sides trying to do that already.

Instead, this book is designed to give you a set of thinking tools so you can reach *your own* conclusion, rather than becoming convinced that my or any other author's conclusion is the right one. It gives you specific techniques for putting together all the facts that have already been thrown at you and combining them with your own values and experiences.

I have come to my own conclusion, of course, but I'll share that with you only as a sort of "sample problem on the blackboard," to demonstrate how the tools can be applied. The last chapter is devoted to giving you a place for assembling your own conclusion by putting together the thinking tools you've learned, the details from the global warming shouting match you've come across, and the values and experiences you bring to the table. Those of you who reach the same conclusion I did will find suggestions in the appendix for how to translate your ideas into action that makes a real difference. If you don't agree with me, you probably won't want my advice anyway. But I've provided resources for you as well.

This is essentially a book about risk management (though it's not as boring as that sounds)—making decisions about what to do in an uncertain situation by estimating risks and payoffs. It's how insurance companies and casinos stay in business despite paying out huge sums of money based on uncertain outcomes, and I suggest we start doing some of that in the global warming debate. Because with either the climate or the economy on the line (depending on which side of the debate you listen to), you've got to admit, the stakes are high.

I know we've all got hectic lives, so I've prepared a handy table to help you decide in a jiffy whether this book is worth your time.

SHOULD I BOTHER TO READ THIS BOOK?
Find yourself in this handy chart.

YOU . . .	READ IT?	WHY?
. . . think global warming is bunk.	Yes	I'm not going to even try to convince you that global warming is real. That said, by the end of the process you may convince *yourself* that we should take drastic action anyway.*
. . . think global warming is a problem but overblown—no way we can affect the whole planet that much.	Yes	You could very well be right. However, while we debate the issue of whether humans can seriously monkey with the climate, we are at the same time running the experiment. The kicker is, no matter what you predict the result of the experiment will be, we're in the test tube. So it's worth making a pretty deliberate bet when the wager may be the whole ball of wax.
. . . think that if global warming were really such a big problem, then they would be dealing with it.	Yes	Have "they" ever messed up before? Hurricane Katrina was a natural disaster, but what happened in New Orleans was a national disgrace. You don't want to look to the crest of the hill for the cavalry in your time of need and hear only crickets. So it may be prudent to do a little looking out for yourself. After all, what's the worst that could happen? You waste a few hours reading a book.

One person who had seen the video this book is based on described himself to me as a staunch Republican, and said that even though he still doesn't believe global warming is true, he now thinks we should take action because it is only prudent to do so.

YOU . . .	READ IT?	WHY?
. . . think global warming is a problem, but there are a ton of *other* environmental causes out there worthy of our limited resources.	Yes	I used to get my shorts in a twist about all sorts of environmental things: old-growth forests, nuclear power, endangered species, blah, blah, blah. But having evaluated climate change with the tools in this book, I've come to think that it simply trumps everything else. Nuclear waste? No problem! Spotted owl? Tastes like chicken! So you might find something interesting in this tale of how I went from a bleeding-heart environmentalist to a harsh pragmatist.
. . . are too busy in life to worry about stuff like this.	Yes	If the American Medical Association said tomorrow, "The color green is bad for you," you might think, "What the heck? Have they gone off their rocker?" But you'd give it a second look. Because they are the most authoritative body in medicine and aren't to be lightly dismissed. Well, what would you think if I told you that the AMA of science has declared that "global warming is a clear threat to society, and we need to act right now"? That doesn't mean you'd believe them. But you'd probably take a second look. Well, they did.[†] Can you really afford to *not* spend a few minutes looking into it?
. . . think global warming is a huge threat and should be addressed immediately, just like a hot poker in the gut.	No[‡]	Don't bother. There are better-researched, more frightening books on the subject if you're looking to wallow in some terror. But one way of addressing global warming is to buy dozens of copies of this book and leave them lying around Laundromats, park benches, your senator's office, and so on. In that case, you'll want to read it first, to make sure you're passing along a good product.

†See *National Academy of Sciences (2005)* and *American Association for the Advancement of Science (2006), pages 108–10.*
‡*So I guess, yes, what I'm saying is that everyone should read this book.*

What's the Worst That Could Happen?

6

Now that you've decided you want to read the book and you're dying to know what makes it so different from all the other "Believe me!/No, believe me!" yellfests, you probably want to dive right in. But hold on there a second—I don't want you bonking your head on any hidden rocks. So I'm going to level with you.

Disclaimer I: I'm No Expert

Let's get one thing clear: I'm not an expert in climate science or economics, the two main fields in the debate. So why on earth should you believe anything I say?

You shouldn't.

I'm really just a Joe Schmo science teacher who's taken an overzealous interest in the subject and who happened to stumble across a way to look at things that seems to have clarified the issue for a lot of people. So instead of focusing on belief, I'm just offering up some thinking tools.

There are already shelves full of better-researched books from experts on both sides of the issue that seem to try to bludgeon you into Belief by Footnote. Take Bjorn Lomborg's *Cool It: The Skeptical Environmentalist's Guide to Global Warming*, almost a full third of which is devoted to notes and references, or Lester Brown's *Plan B 3.0: Mobilizing to Save Civilization*, which is like a tight race between academic-prose-induced sleepiness and wide-awake terror—each time I pick it up, I don't know whether I'm going to end up falling asleep or running around the block, flailing my arms. That's why I won't try to convince you to believe what I say. I think focusing so much on believing or not believing is part of what has us paralyzed in the debate.

This issue is not about the question, Should I *believe* global warming is true? any more than starting your car is about the question, Should I *believe* I'm going to get into a wreck this trip? It's simply not a useful question because the answer cannot be known for sure. Until you actually run the experiment, that is.

Instead, the real question—the one that we unconsciously ask ourselves all the time—is, What should I do right now, given the risks and uncertainties? In the car, for instance, it boils down to, Do I buckle my seatbelt? That depends on a quick balancing of the hassles and risks involved. Does it buckle itself at the touch of a button and give you a nice massage in the process? Or is the end buried down in the seat crack among chewing gum and razor blades? Are you going for a lazy Sunday drive? Or are you going to speed along a twisty, narrow, icy road—in the dark—through a herd of moose? With lots of blind corners. And locusts.

> **This book doesn't focus on *what* to think about global warming but on *how* to think about global warming. In that way, you can come up with a conclusion all your own, without having to buy into what anybody says.**

As a science teacher, I have come to have a lot more faith in the *process* of critical thinking than I have in what any particular person tells me. So it would warm my heart if you were a critical reader. In fact, I expect you to challenge what I say. Google it. Make notes in the margins. Poke at it. Pick it up and swing it around a bit, see if you like the heft of it. (Try not to hit anything.) If it's handy, then use it. If not, then all you've lost is a couple hours out of the 657,000 or so given to most of us in our lifetimes.

I'll even start you off, like this.

Skepticism is good. You're right to be skeptical of people who want you to change your life, or your government's policies, or your oil. But like with so many good things—vitamin C, sunlight, playing World of Warcraft online—too much of a good thing can be harmful to you. Knee-jerk skepticism is as damaging as none at all. If you go overboard, you just end up sounding like that Monty Python skit about the argument clinic: "Aw, this isn't even an argument!" "Yes, it is!" "No, it isn't!" The tools in this book are intended to help you use your skepticism to your advantage, by being deliberate with it.

And you should know that because the whole timeline thing has me nervous, I chose to write this book in just 15 weeks. As a result, I didn't have time to do all the reading and research I would have liked. In that sense it's a bit like what the activists are claiming about global warming—we may not have time to wait for the "perfect" answer, so "good enough for now" is better than nothing. Keep in mind that I am offering suggestions on how to think rather than facts I claim to be true. I expect a critical reader, like you, to look up my claims anyway.

> A handy benefit of this disclaimer is that if you discover an error, I can say, "I left that there on purpose, as a test for critical readers. Good job catching it."

Disclaimer 2: I'm Biased

When it comes to the issue of global climate change, I'll admit that I have a huge bias. Two, actually. Their names are Katie and Alex. The welfare of my two young daughters dominates all of my decision making, and on any issue that might involve their welfare, I have a strong bias for making decisions that leave large safety margins.

And frankly, what I've learned about the possible size and speed of climate change scares the bejee- sus out of me. I think about what it may do to my girls' lives, and I feel like running around buying up cultivable land and sil- ver coins in case civilization falls.

> I may be wrong. In fact, I really hope I am. But I'm not going to count on it.

So I'm desperate to break the deadlock in the debate.

Rather than do that by trying to manipulate you, I'm providing some common tools that both sides can use to debate the issue instead of continuing to shout past each other. I've done my best to propose the thinking tools in this book in as objective and evenhanded a way as I can, though I know everyone makes that claim.

> Whether I have succeeded or not is for you to decide. Either way, perhaps at least some of what I suggest here will be useful to you.

To check the ways in which my bias might have influenced the thinking tools I suggest in this book, I contacted over 200 authors, thinkers, policy makers, and scientists involved in the global warming debate. I asked them to critique my suggested tools and tell me if they thought I was being fair. The main criticism I got back was that *both* sides—skeptics and activists alike—thought that I went too easy on the other guys. How's that for finding the middle ground? *No one* likes me!

Just how did I get so universally disliked? Well, that's another story.

That Other Story

Since attending a particular chemistry lecture back in the 1990s, I have been thinking about climate change literally every day. Mulling the issue for so long and growing fatigued

> Thanks a bundle, Professor Gammon.

at how we seemed to be chasing our tails in the public debate, I found myself toying with a standard logic tool—the decision grid—to see if it could clarify things at all.

The first time I drew this little 2×2 grid and put climate change into it, the answer to the debate popped right out, seemingly undeniable. It was suddenly clear that we were deadlocked because *we had been asking the wrong question*, one that

> This is what Chapter I is about.

GLOBAL WARMING	ACTION	
	A Significant Action Now	**B** Little to No Action Now
False		
True		

The decision grid.

relied on eliminating the uncertainty about whether dangerous human-caused global warming is real or not before making a decision about what (if anything) we should do about it. The amazing thing is the grid allows the issue to be decided *despite* the uncertainties!

I was stunned. It was a weird "How come I've never heard of this?" sort of moment, because with the grid there was simply no need to decide which side of the debate to believe. It was like a Magical Grid Machine that took uncertainty and turned it into confidence almost effortlessly.

The debate was over not because I'd found a way to show which side was right but because I'd found a way to show that the debate *itself* was moot. The real question about dangerous global warming is not, Is it true? but, Is it worth doing anything about, just in case it's true?

In a sort of megalomaniacal way, it felt a little like the universe had chosen me to give The Answer to. But it was dif-

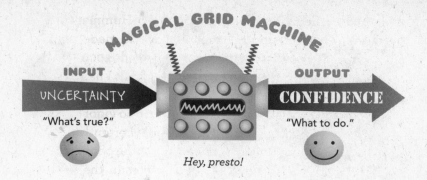

MAGICAL GRID MACHINE

INPUT
UNCERTAINTY
"What's true?"

OUTPUT
CONFIDENCE
"What to do."

Hey, presto!

ficult to express it in words alone; whenever I tried, I always needed to snatch whatever paper was handy and sketch it out. Because the argument was inherently visual and couldn't be given effectively by speaking or writing, there was no means for me to get the word out in any significant way. Some Answer.

Thanks a bundle, Universe.

When my wife and I finally got high-speed Internet in 2007, I spent some time on YouTube to see what all the ruckus was about. It quickly dawned on me that *this* was the way to spread my answer: a visual medium, with the bonus of having the potential for reaching a ton of people all at once. So in spring 2007, I posted "The Most Terrifying Video You'll Ever See" (a title suggested by my students) on YouTube. The 10-minute video of me at a whiteboard talking about global warming immediately went viral, ending up right next to Britney Spears and skateboarding accidents as a most-popular video. Who says life isn't surprising?

The argument seemed undeniable to me, but I figured the last time someone was infallible was a couple thousand years ago. So to find the shortcomings in my thinking, I challenged viewers of the video to poke holes in my argument. The response was ... uh ... spirited. Turns out my "undeniable" argument had a hole in it big enough to drive a Hummer through because of an assumption I hadn't realized I'd made.

Isn't that just the way with assumptions? Douglas Adams wrote: "The most devilish assumptions are the ones you don't realize you have."

Four million views and 8,000 critical comments later, I felt I had developed really good patches for all the holes that had been so vigorously poked. I had inadvertently compiled all the details of the popular debate—what you hear in the news, on blogs, and around the water cooler—and found that, when run through the grid, they

After we construct the grid in Chapter 1, we'll blow it apart.

Again!

stacked up to what really seemed to be a watertight analysis.

Now that I really did have The Answer to one of the biggest debates in history, I couldn't just hold on to it. But from making the video I'd already racked up a huge time debt to my wife and daughters. I had to get this thing out of my hands and get back to my family as soon as possible. So over the course of six maniacal weeks, with almost no sleep, hopped up on Red Bull and Little Caesars pizza, I produced a series of 52 more videos, attempting to answer every single question, objection, concern, "You missed a spot," and "Yeah, but" that I had been able to find.

The Project (as it came to be known in my house) was my magnum opus, my midlife crisis, my nervous breakdown, and my enlightenment experience all rolled into one. Yet despite adding silly hats and explosions, the new, improved video, titled "How It All Ends," never got

Sounds like a fun time!

anywhere near the attention that the original one (with its flawed argument) did. But at least I had gotten the darn thing out of my hands.

In the ensuing months, I got requests for collaborations prompted by the success of the original video—a book here, a short TV spot there, websites all over the place, professors

Should I Bother to Read This Book?

using my videos in classes, students wanting help with the assignments from those same professors—but I just said no to all. Clearly I had struck a nerve, but I finished The Project to get it out of me, and now I needed to go back to being a father and a husband and a teacher.

So how did I end up suffering even more sleep-deprived nights and family-deprived days to get this book written? The reason I'm still trying to get my silly little grid out to as many people as possible is that the potential catastrophic destabilization of the climate—and all the effects that cascade from that—may quite feasibly destroy my children's standard of living, their health, and perhaps their very survival. Sounds extreme, doesn't it?

The Bottom Line

I'm going to say something that's probably going to tick off some folks on the political left. The recent warnings from some well-established scientists are now so dire that, to me, this issue is no longer about being good for the environment or saving the planet or even the welfare of future generations. It is about safeguarding the stability of my environment in the immediate future—as in the physical surroundings that affect the quality of life for my daughters as they grow up.

Remember: Doesn't mean they're true. It just means they're on the table.

So this is ultimately selfish. It is about me and mine and our security, about protecting us from the perils of the future. Many people see global warming as a political issue. Al Gore called it a moral issue. Freeman Dyson called it a religious issue (the "secular religion of environmentalism"). I disagree with all of them.

To me, this is—plain and simple—an issue of security. It's no longer about saving the planet—it's about saving our bacon.

Because in my survey of the subject, I've glimpsed an unlikely but feasible future where I end up holding people off at gunpoint to protect my grandkids' clean drinking water, due to a breakdown of modern civilization triggered by sudden and irreversible climate destabilization.

I'll do that if it comes to it. But I'd really rather not.

I used to care about saving the world, but now I just want to safeguard my daughters. I want to do all that I reasonably can to eliminate the small possibility of that nightmare scenario. And this book is my selfish attempt to do that—by spurring the world to safeguard itself. So, in the end, this pursuit is not idealistic or environmental or aesthetic. It is simply pragmatic. I'm writing this book so that you—yes, *you* holding this book—will go out and change the course of history, to make life less harsh for me and my kids in the future.

So yes, fine—it turns out I *am* trying to manipulate you for my own ends. If it's any consolation, I think it will probably make the future better for you and your family, too.

In summary, here's what you'll find in this book:

- Some easy but powerful tools for answering the biggest question of our time: When given contradictory statements from experts about a complex but possibly imminent doomsday scenario, what's a harried lay person supposed to do?

- A tried-and-tested method for dealing with the uncertainty and coming to *your own conclusion* with confidence. I'll present the tools as objectively as I can and then demonstrate their use by showing you how I used them to draw my conclusion. You'll get a do-it-yourself chapter, with prompts to help you reach a personal decision.

- Strategies for putting your conclusion into action—if it matches mine. (If it doesn't match mine, then you'll probably be sick of listening to my yammering anyway.) Suggested actions are stunningly easy, immensely powerful, surprisingly comprehensive, and tailor-made to your life. (Wow! Do you get a free set of knives, too?) And they have nothing to do with buying those little twirly lightbulbs.

- A chance to tell me directly at www .gregcraven.org where you think I missed a spot or made yet another unknowing assumption. You can also share the conclusions you draw from this book with others and debate the topic using thinking tools common to both sides. It will be a nice change from the usual online flame wars over this topic.

One mistake closer to truth is how I see it whenever I discover I'm wrong. But jeez, it's taking a while to get there.

- *Bonus, at no extra cost!* While the specific information about global warming will change rapidly (perhaps the doomsday will be called off or perhaps you'll already be under water as you read this), the thinking tools given here will never go out of date. You can apply them to *any* difficult decision you are faced with, especially if the shoutfest shifts from, Should we do something about climate change? to, What exactly should we do?

- A refreshingly different take on an environmental issue. You've heard of the Skeptical Environmentalist? Well, I'm the Green Realist. Because I say forget the planet—save *us*!

That's a bumper sticker you'll never see!

So, are you along for the ride?

CHAPTER 1

THE DECISION GRID:
WHAT'S THE WORST THAT COULD HAPPEN?
(OR GIANT MUTANT SPACE HAMSTERS)

Now that you've decided to read this book, I've got your first homework assignment for you. This will turn out to be important, so don't procrastinate.

I heard that groan. I'm a high school teacher— don't think I'm not used to it.

The topic at hand is global warming. For now, we'll take *global warming* to mean "human activities such as burning coal and oil are putting enough carbon dioxide into the atmosphere to cause the planet to warm up, and that's going to be a bad thing for us." There are other takes on the term (such as simply "the globe is warming," without referring to humans, or "humans are warming the globe, but it will be an overall good thing"). But for our purposes, we'll address the most controversial version—that humans are screwing up the planet with all the fossil fuel burning. Properly, that's called "dangerous human-caused global warming," but that gets tiresome to read, so I will generally just use *global warming* throughout the book to mean the same thing.

Or "dangerous anthropogenic global warming," in geekspeak.

Here's your assignment: Before you read this chapter, take a minute to pause and think in some detail about your current opinion on global warming. Perhaps you think it is the biggest boondoggle in history, and the Chicken Littles should be strung up by their thumbs. Perhaps you think it is the biggest threat in human history, and we should pull out all the stops to fight it ASAP. Perhaps you're somewhere in the middle but inclined more toward one side than the other.

So here's the question for you to answer: What would you have to see for your opinion to change?

IF YOU ARE INCLINED TO THINK GLOBAL WARMING IS OVERBLOWN . . .	IF YOU ARE INCLINED TO BE CONCERNED ABOUT GLOBAL WARMING AND THINK WE SHOULD DO SOMETHING ABOUT IT . . .
What would you have to see for you to become convinced that we should take *massive* action right now to combat global warming?	What would you have to see for you to become convinced that we should *not* do *anything* right now to fight it?

Take some time to come up with a description of the conditions that would change your mind, and then write them inside the back cover of this book. This is a critical exercise. I've found that if I can't come up with even an inkling of how my mind might be changed, then I'm not really thinking at all; I'm just set on holding on to my current beliefs. And because I'm probably not perfect yet, sometimes I act on a wrong understanding and end up shooting myself in the foot. Better to find my errors before they find me.

Plus, if you can't come up with some picture that would change your mind, you shouldn't waste time reading this book. Because you already know what your opinion will be at the end (you can't imagine a way for it to be changed), there's really nothing to see here. You can put the book down and spend your time doing things that are way more fun.

So write the conditions for changing your mind in the back of the book before you read on. No cheating.

Confidence from Chaos

The two sides in the shouting match are so far apart, they don't even seem to be on the same planet. We need a way to sort through this mess without requiring a PhD

Did you do it yet?

or hundreds of hours of slogging through techno-jargon in the scientific literature.

How about saying, "The truth is probably somewhere in the middle"? That often works, but in science it's rarely the case, because one explanation usually ends up being much closer to the truth than the other. And anyway, with stakes this high, we deserve something a little more thorough than a cliché and shrug of the shoulders.

You hear some East Coast intellectual say, "Global warming will cause ecosystem collapses that will completely gut U.S. agriculture." And that scares you. But then you hear some other egghead say, "It still isn't even proven that increases in CO_2 cause increases in temperature." And then you feel calm again. In this back and forth, here's one thing to remember: Just because a smart person says something, *it doesn't mean it's true*. We're all human. We all make mistakes.

So what do you do if you can't believe what anybody says, no matter how smart he or she seems?

That's where the Magical Grid Machine comes in. It allows you to stop waiting for certainty and instead make a decision right now by sketching out the different possibili-

In fact, in Chapter 3 I'll show how we've all been issued defective brains—you and me included. It's a hoot!

ties for the future. That way—because there is always a chance you could be wrong—you can compare possible outcomes and decide which risks you would prefer to run. The clever part is that it changes the question from, Who should I believe? to, What should I do? After all, the physical world is unaffected by our *beliefs*. It reacts only to our *actions*. So the grid allows you to stop focusing on who's right and instead ask, *What's the wisest thing to do, given the risks and consequences?*

Here's how it works:

The first factor in the decision grid is whether global warming is real or not. So we set up a row for each possibility: true

GLOBAL WARMING	ACTION	
	A **Significant Action Now**	**B** **Little to No Action Now**
False		
True		

The decision grid.

and false. We can sidestep that whole contentious question of whether the globe is warming or not and whether we're the ones doing it by acknowledging that no one is perfect and that there are two basic possibilities. No one can predict with absolute certainty what the physical world will or will not do, and all reasonable people should be able to admit that there's a chance they might have a mistaken understanding. So we all agree—even the most panicked activist and the most hardened skeptic—that the top row and the bottom row are both possibilities.

This admission that any of us might be wrong is what changes the question from, Who's right in the shouting match? to, What's the most reasonable thing to do? This is how we get to extract ourselves from the tar pit that this debate has become. After all, as humans, we can never be completely certain about the future; so asking yourself, What if I'm wrong? and building a little bit of a plan B into your decisions can only serve you well.

Hurray!

The other factor is whether we decide to take significant action now. This gives us two columns: A for significant action now and B for little to no significant action now.

Exactly what <u>action</u> means, we'll cover in Chapter 5. For now, take it as "reduce carbon dioxide emissions."

The result is four boxes, each one representing a different future scenario. This allows us to trace out the possible consequences of the choices we make now and compare the outcomes side by side. Then we can decide which risks we'd rather run.

What might each of these futures look like?

First is the future in which we took action and global warming turned out not to be real after all—the *top left* box. That would represent a mistake on our part. What might be the consequences of that? Wasted money, mostly, plus reduced liberties (new limits on consumer choices, stricter land-use laws, and so on). This is what the skeptics warn us about. Increased taxation, oppressive regulations, bloated government.

For the purposes of contrast, let's be really pessimistic and take things to the extreme. What's the worst that could happen if we took action and didn't need to? Let's say there are massive layoffs caused by draconian regulations and runaway government spending, sparking a severe recession that collapses the U.S. dollar and destroys the international banking system, plunging the entire world into a depression that makes the 1930s look like a cakewalk.

That box deserves a frowny face.

In the *top right* box is the future in which we didn't take action and it turned out we didn't need to. We made the right decision. Everybody celebrates: the skeptics because they were right and the activists because it wasn't the end of the world after all. We get continued prosperity, with no big economic consequences.

	ACTION	
GLOBAL WARMING	**A** **Significant Action Now**	**B** **Little to No Action Now**
False	Global depression 	
True		

In the *bottom left* box is the future in which we took action—and it was a good thing because the doomsayers were right. The carbon hit the fan, but we made the right decision and prevented a doomsday. This turned out to be the right choice. We've still got the direct economic costs associated with taking action, but because the modern financial system

	ACTION	
GLOBAL WARMING	**A** **Significant Action Now**	**B** **Little to No Action Now**
False	Global depression 	Party!
True		

| GLOBAL WARMING | ACTION | |
	A **Significant Action Now**	B **Little to No Action Now**
False	Global depression	Party!
True	Economic costs Increased regulations But worth it!	

hinges so much on confidence and psychology (remember how investor fear tanked the stock market during the financial meltdown of October 2008?), the system didn't collapse; people saw the expenditures as worthwhile. People may have griped about the rationing during World War II, but all agreed it was worth it in the end. So even though there's still significant cost involved, let's give that box a neutral face, because it could have been a lot worse.

In fact, cloth rationing during World War II led to the invention of the bikini! Necessity is the mother of invention after all.

That leaves the *bottom right* box. This is the future in which the doomsayers were right, but we listened to the skeptics and didn't take significant action in time. That's the second possible mistake in our grid. If we took a pessimistic view of the other mistake—the top left box—then we should do the same thing in the bottom right. This is where it gets really ugly, with all the Gloomy Gus disaster fantasies that you hear about: sea levels rising 20 feet, droughts, storms, floods, famine, epidemics, and the collapse of a global economy battered by nonstop disaster. A world that makes Al Gore

Yada, yada, yada.

look like an overly optimistic sissy with no guts who sugar-coated the bad news. Frowny face for sure.

But because the economic collapse in the bottom right box would incorporate everything in the economic collapse of the top left box (with an economy destroyed by all the chaos) *plus* all the bonus features of natural disasters, it seems appropriate to upgrade that frowny face to a full-on grimace.

GLOBAL WARMING	ACTION	
	A Significant Action Now	**B** Little to No Action Now
False	Global depression 😦	Party! 😊
True	Economic costs Increased regulations But worth it! 😐	Global catastrophe (economic, social, political, public health, environmental) 😵

Making a Choice

> Did the smiley faces give that away?

Obviously, this is grossly simplified. But for a first pass through, this can be useful, and we can say that our future will fall roughly into one of those four boxes.

In using the grid to analyze our choices, it might be useful to distinguish between "row thinking" and "column thinking." In the uproar over global warming, we have been preoccupied almost entirely with row thinking—that is, trying to predict which row the future will fall into. These are the questions we have been mired in: Are the doomsday predictions true or not? Which row is the correct one?

However, we can never know the absolute truth about the physical world, so we can't know for certain which row we'll end up in. Until we arrive there. What we *can* know for certain—because we control it—is which *column* the future will be in. With row thinking, we're stuck with *guessing* about our future, because the rows depend on the laws of physics, which we can't control. With column thinking, we get a *choice* about our future, because the columns depend on our actions, which we can control. Doesn't that sound better?

We're still studying the law of gravity, for Pete's sake! More on that in Chapter 2.

Using the grid gives you back the power you may feel you've lost—How am I supposed to decide what's true when all the experts are shouting opposite things?—a feeling that has caused many people to just throw up their hands and ignore the whole mess. You can breathe a sigh of relief because the grid changes the question from, Is global warming really going to be a problem? (which we can't know for sure until it happens or not) to the much more accessible, Given the risks and uncertainties, what seems like the best bet? That question, even we non-PhDs can handle.

Educated guesses, to be fair. But we're still essentially trying to predict the future.

It's a bit like buying a lottery ticket. (Well, a mandatory lottery. No opting out as long as you're on the planet. But you do get a choice.) Today we choose ticket A or ticket B, each with a set of two scenarios. This narrows down the possible future scenarios to two basic options—the ones in the column of our choice. And then we wait until time and the laws of physics scratch off the uncertainty to reveal which row (and, therefore, which box) we end up in.

"Sorry, you are not a winner. Please play again." D'oh!

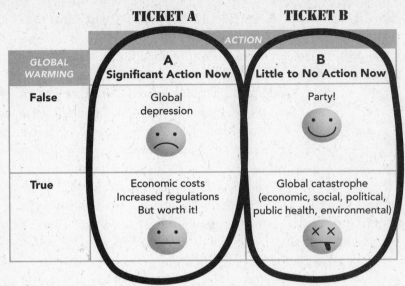

	TICKET A	TICKET B
	ACTION	
GLOBAL WARMING	**A** Significant Action Now	**B** Little to No Action Now
False	Global depression	Party!
True	Economic costs Increased regulations But worth it!	Global catastrophe (economic, social, political, public health, environmental)

Choose a lottery ticket.

You probably don't realize it, but we use this thinking unconsciously all the time. We are constantly making choices based on unknown future outcomes. For instance, say that all day long you've been craving a roast beef sandwich with all the fixings. When you get home and prepare it, you're bummed to find that the mayonnaise got left out overnight. Do you put it on your sandwich or not? Into each box of the grid go the consequences (the costs and benefits) of that possible future scenario.

You balance how likely it is that the mayo has gone bad with how much you've looked forward to the sandwich (how disappointed will those sad faces really be?).

Sniff, sniff.

In a slightly less mundane example, every time you get in the car, you make an unconscious decision about whether to buckle your seatbelt or not. You may not be aware of it, but you do a quick weighing of the costs and benefits of doing so.

ACTION: EAT IT?		
MAYO HAS GONE BAD	**A** Yes	**B** No
False	Yum! 	Disappointed
True	Blarch! 	Disappointed

Mayo grid.

If you play with this kind of grid for a while, you'll notice that it usually comes down to comparing two different types of errors and deciding which kind you would prefer to risk: having acted when it turns out you didn't need to (in the seat-

ACTION: BUCKLE UP?		
END UP IN A WRECK	**A** Yes	**B** No
False	Some hassle buckling it Turns out it wasn't useful 	No time wasted buckling, so save 3 seconds Marginally happier
True	Some hassle buckling it You're so glad you did! 	In hindsight, the hassle of buckling seems trivial

Seatbelt grid.

belt example, the top left) or *not* having acted when it turns out you *did* need to (the bottom right).

The Choice Is Obvious(ly Rigged)

If you look again at the grid on global warming, the choice between lottery tickets seems quite clear. Sure, we'd like to go for the top right box because it's the only happy face in the whole grid. But choosing the ticket that contains the smiley face would run the danger of ending up in the bottom right—clearly an unacceptable gamble. Especially when that losing outcome is contrasted with the comparatively mild danger associated with choosing ticket A—the top left box. The risk of a global depression is nothing to be sniffed at, but it is clearly preferable to the risk of a global depression in the midst of constant natural catastrophes, epidemics, and resource wars.

> No do-overs on a dead planet.

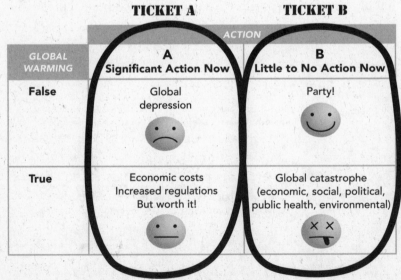

Again with the lottery tickets.

When framed like this, it is easy to answer the question, Which is the greater risk: taking action or not taking action? Obviously, the only rational decision is to choose column A, to eliminate the possibility of the bottom right box in column B. It really is like making a bet, and in column B you're wagering the world. Who wants that on their résumé?

When I was first developing this grid with my classes and we realized it was like placing a bet, some students got excited to try it. Tania was first and chose column B. I flipped the coin, and she landed in the bottom right. The next student stepped up to play, but then it dawned on us that you get to lose that bet only once. Tania had destroyed the world, so no one else got to play. I heard "<u>Great job</u>, Tania!" the rest of the day.

Well, drawing that conclusion is where my unconscious assumption sank my first video, because that's where I stopped. But if you play with the grid some more, you see that it would argue for action to guard against *any* potential danger, no matter how ridiculous the threat or how expensive the action. Simply insert any wildly speculative and really dangerous-sounding threat into the grid in place of global warming, and you'll see that the grid comes to the same conclusion—that we should do everything possible to stop that threat. Even if it's something like giant mutant space hamsters (GMSHs). Because it's better to go broke building a fleet of orbiting rodent traps than it is to risk even the *possibility* of becoming hamster chow, right? After all, what's the worst that could happen in each case? Clearly, the risk of not taking action is far worse than the risk of taking action. Just look at that hamster!

Go ahead—try your own ridiculous scenario! It's fun!

After people poked this hole (the one big enough to drive a Hummer through) in my "The Most Terrifying

On page 30.

	ACTION	
GMSHs	**A** **Significant Action Now**	**B** **Little to No Action Now**
False	Economic costs	Status quo
True	Economic costs But saved our bacon!	Hamster Chow!

How to break the idea of the grid.

Video You'll Ever See," I realized that I had assumed that the likelihood of catastrophic global warming was far more credible than the risk of GMSHs. An assumption, I discovered, not shared by everyone.

In fact, more than a few viewers of the video suggested that I should never leave my home because the grid would argue that that's better than the risk of getting hit by lightning. It's nice to know they had my interests in mind.

As long as disaster is threatened in the bottom right box, the grid argues for action. Everyone's got to admit that they can't know the future for certain—who are they to say for sure that the hamsters don't exist? So we go broke guarding against every conceivable threat. Using such a grid, apparently, is pointless.

And while we're piling on, how do we know that the disaster scenarios in the global warming grid would be so horrendous? Maybe the world represented by the bottom right grimace wouldn't turn out to be so bad after all; maybe we'd see only mild changes and perhaps even some positives, such as extended growing seasons and fewer deaths in the winter from cold. Or maybe the top left outcome symbolized by the frowny face would actually turn out to be better captured by a smiley, with energy independence for the United States (no more playing global oil cop), tons of dough made by selling renewable energy technology to the up-and-coming Chinese middle class (since we were the early adopters), and greater homeland security due to a decentralized energy infrastructure more resistant to terrorist attack. Sounds like a party!

Or maybe the "winning" scenarios in the grid wouldn't be as happy as we've assumed: Perhaps global warming turns out to be true but our attempted remedies have no effect, so the bottom left neutral face turns positively ugly because we end up with a climate catastrophe *and* we're too broke to adapt to it. Or maybe the top right box won't be so full of giggles after all because we soon run out of fossil fuels anyway, and the United States ends up importing most of its energy from renewable sources in Mexico (sunny) and Canada (watery), who got a head start on developing alternative energy infrastructures. Plus population growth is an Exponential Fun Zone that's going to ruin the party in the future of the top right box sooner or later.

> If you're thinking to yourself, "But we've got plenty of coal for the next 500 years," you'll want to see the video by Albert A. Bartlett mentioned in the notes on page 187.

So the Magical Grid Machine appears to have gotten us nowhere.

> So . . . why are you reading this book again? See the chart in Chapter 0.

Great. You Broke It. Now What?

After "The Most Terrifying Video You'll Ever See" hit the web, I was left with a great idea gutted by critical examination. But that's good. That's how we make ideas better—by trying to poke holes in them and then finding ways to fix the holes. As

I read and responded to the thousands of criticisms in the months following the video's viral explosion, the various holes and patches fell into place.

The grid is intended to break the paralysis caused by waiting for the perfect answer before committing to a decision by changing the question from, What is the correct answer? to, What seems like the best bet? But it doesn't break the paralysis in its present form because it would argue for drastic action against every imagined threat.

However, the grid can provide a relatively clear answer when we take into consideration probabilities. For example, if the top row is way more likely to occur than the bottom row, then we can move the line dividing the rows down to provide a visual sense of their relative likelihood. This can make the attractiveness of column B over column A pretty clear. Take, for example, the more reasonable assessment that GMSHs are extremely unlikely to be real.

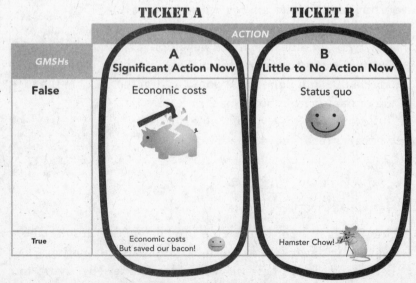

How to fix the grid you just broke.

When we move the horizontal line so the sizes of the grid's boxes reflect the relative probability of GMSHs being real, the grid once again gives an answer that is in line with common sense—preparing for the unlikely event of a rodent invasion is not worth the huge cost of doing so.

And as we saw for the global warming grid on page 28, if the relative likelihoods of the rows being correct are equal, a matter of a simple coin toss, the better bet can still be clear when the mistake in one column is way worse than the mistake in the other.

So you can see that there are two factors that determine which column is preferable:

- The **likelihood** of the rows (probabilities).
- The **contents** of the boxes (consequences or risks).

There are mathematical ways to evaluate these (as well as all the intermediate cases), like game theory and the expected value function in statistics. But we'll leave those to the textbooks. And Wikipedia.

But trying to determine those would seem to put us right back at the mercy of the eggheads and pundits. How else are you supposed to figure out what the possibilities are except by reading and listening? My promise to give you refuge from the shouting match has fallen apart, and it seems like I'm just going to throw you back in.

I am indeed proposing just that. But before you wade back in, you'll equip yourself with some specific tools that will help you extract some sense from the noise, which you can then use to create a grid that works:

- An understanding of the **nature of science**, which will allow you to put aside a ton of concerns about the likelihood of the rows.

Forewarned is forearmed.

- An awareness of all the devilish **traps that your mind sets for you**, so that you can avoid them.

- A method for evaluating the **relative credibility** of what you hear, so that you can weigh conflicting statements against each other.

I have found these tools to be immensely helpful in preventing me from getting overwhelmed by the onslaught of opinions, references, studies, petitions, and blog postings that churn around global warming. Armed with these tools, you can wade confidently back into the shouting match and come out with your quarry: the likelihood of the rows and the expected contents of the boxes. Then you can build a grid that is valid and useful, one that can give you a confident answer to the question, What seems like the wisest course to take right now? It also helps to remember that you don't need to come out with certainty, just relative likelihood. The grid can then provide you with confidence.

That is what the remainder of the book is about: giving you these tools so that you can face the shouting match and draw your own conclusions, without having to rely on mine. As mentioned in Chapter 0, I will share my conclusion and show you how I arrived at it, but my ultimate aim is for you to use the tools to draw your own conclusion. So the last chapter is a template with space for you to do just that. Like homework, but you won't have to turn it in for a grade.

Or, at least, I won't be doing the grading. I guess the physical world will be doing it for us all.

Repeat After Me . . .

To save you some time, later in the book I will devote considerable time to the main arguments from both sides of the debate.

I suggest you go looking elsewhere for information as well. Don't just trust that I've presented things fairly. You don't even know me. I may be a shady character.

As you progress through the book, there is one point to keep in mind at all times because it is critically important: You will continually find yourself falling back into the temptation of trying to figure out which side is correct. But you don't need to know who's right any more than you need to know what the next dice roll will be to place a decent bet. To help you keep your eye on the prize, I recommend you write the following mantra in red ink in the top margin every time you turn a page:

I don't need to determine who is right to make a decent bet.

Life is complicated and imprecise. We all want to know what is correct or right, but for an issue as complex as global warming, intertwined with a field no one seems to be able to get right (economics), I suggest that you are better off having some tolerance for uncertainty and instead go for the big picture. That's what the tools in this book are designed to help you do.

It's only natural to want to get "just the facts," but they aren't always clear at the time a bet is required. That's basic risk management, and I think it would serve us well to start using it with global warming.

But First: A Word About Words

I like to refer to people by the terms they themselves use. It keeps things more civil. So, although you'll hear the terms *alarmist* and *denialist* used in the debate to refer to those who advocate column A and column B, respectively, I'm going to refer to them throughout this book as *warmers* and *skeptics* because that's how I've heard them refer to themselves. For me, there is no value judgment implied by either term.

There are two basic camps that I'm lumping into skeptics for the time being—those who claim that human-caused global warming is insignificant and those who say that it is significant but that the best way to address it is through adapting to the changes rather than trying to prevent them. What both camps under the skeptic label share is an opposition to pursuing significant cuts in carbon emissions; they both advocate column B as the better choice. We'll explore the distinction in more depth as it becomes important.

For the time being, if someone *opposes* the statement "We should take significant action to cut carbon dioxide emissions to reduce the amount of global warming," then he or she is a skeptic. If someone *agrees* with that statement, he or she is a warmer. So my definitions of *warmer* and *skeptic* really come down to enthusiasm for cutting carbon dioxide emissions.

And, while the terms *global warming* and *global climate change* actually refer to different (but closely related) phenomena, for the purposes of this book I'm going to use them interchangeably. Sometimes I may even refer to the issue as the Global Climate Hoedown.

Not really.

You've probably heard a bunch of terms that all seem to be used to mean the same thing, such as *greenhouse gases, carbon emissions, carbon dioxide, carbon,* and *CO_2 levels.* For now, I'll use all these to mean "the stuff going in the air that's got the warmers all in a fuss," and we'll sort the rest out in Chapter 8.

I will refer to two separate debates on global warming: the popular debate and the scientific debate. The *popular* debate on global warming is what you are exposed to through news magazines, newspapers, talk radio, TV news, blogs, and forwarded email. The *scientific* debate is what the scientists are saying to each other, and this goes on in places that most lay people (myself included) don't have easy access to and wouldn't be able to follow if they did: peer-reviewed journals and scientific conferences. Geekland.

One of the big topics in the popular debate is whether there really is much of a scientific debate going on. It seems a key point (Do most of the scientists agree on this or not?), but the lay person's only indication of what's going on in the scientific debate is what gets reported in the popular debate, which is filled with spin. If I were to tell you, "Hey, trust me, the scientific debate is over," then I'd just be another voice in the shouting match, and you would have no reason to believe me. Thus, we're not even going to concern ourselves with the scientific debate in this book. Your plight is the popular debate, so that is what I'm going to equip you for.

When's the last time you attended a climate change conference? Me neither.

And the first piece of equipment is an understanding of how science works.

CHAPTER 2

THE NATURE OF SCIENCE:
WE NEVER QUITE KNOW FOR SURE

First up in the tool kit: understanding a little bit about the nature of science. This is necessary because it lays critical groundwork for evaluating the credibility of statements you hear as you go about trying to determine the likelihood of the rows and the contents of the boxes in your grid. We'll build on this in Chapter 4. As a convenient side effect, understanding how science works also dislodges us from several very reasonable concerns that the debate often gets hung up on, like:

Like in Chapters 6 and 7.

- Why not just wait until the science is settled?
- The human impact on global warming hasn't been proven.
- The scientists keep changing their minds—back in the '70s they were warning of a coming ice age—so why listen to them now?
- Why should we base our future on the results of a few computer climate models?

Proof Is in the Eye of the Beholder

It's only natural to wonder, Why not just wait until the science is settled? Then we'll *know* what to do. After all, we are talking about potentially tremendous outlays of money and huge changes in policy. None of us wants to spend a ton of energy and money unless we absolutely need to. Nobody would object to diverting resources to dealing with an oncoming asteroid.

Although some argue that taking action will actually have a net economic benefit, as we'll see in Chapter 6.

But the threat here isn't that obvious, so why not study it more until it is?

There are two problems with that way of thinking. We saw the first in Chapter 0—the 100,000-volt buzzer that may be attached to the room we're all in as we watch the debate run its course.

And the other problem is the nature of science itself. The way the debate is currently framed—Is human-caused global warming true, or not? Is it severe, or not? Will our actions have a significant effect, or not?—simply asks science for something that it cannot, by its very nature, ever provide: certainty.

As a science teacher, I can tell you that science—that most precise and geeky of all human endeavors—is surprisingly *never* certain. Every single scientific statement carries with it some sort of estimate of how big the uncertainty is, because it is simply part of science to admit explicitly that neither you nor your instruments are perfect. Surprisingly, this means there will almost always be some disagreement on *any* scientific question.

On the face of it, this sounds like a ridiculous claim. If scientific answers are never certain, then how come we rely on them all the time? Why do we trust science enough to take its medicines and fly in its airplanes and work in its skyscrapers? We trust science because as it goes on, it works to make the uncertainty attached to its answers smaller and smaller, until the uncertainty is small enough for the task at hand. So saying "We shouldn't take action on X until the remaining uncertainty is dispelled" is a bit like saying "You shouldn't leave your home until you know for absolute certain that you won't get struck by lightning." It's silly. You just need the uncertainty to be small enough that the benefits of leaving your home outweigh the risks.

But if it were true that science is never certain, wouldn't that contradict the idea of scientific proof?

Yes. Yes, it would. Here's a staggering fact not commonly understood: Science can never *prove* anything.

Listen. I'm not a real scientist. But I play one in my classroom. I can get away with saying things that are my best guess when my audience is 35 teenagers. But before I decided to make such a bold claim in a book reaching, um, more than 35 people, I figured I had better double-check. I could always be wrong. So I contacted some real scientists, and those who got back to me confirmed my understanding.

> They could be wrong, too. But for what it's worth, they are way more qualified than I am.

Here's a representative view, from Donald Langenberg, who's not only a *real* scientist but is also respected enough by his peers to have been elected as the president of the American Association for the Advancement of Science. After saying that he's not an expert in the logic of science (this cautiousness is another aspect of science!), he noted:

> AAAS is the largest scientific society in the world. More on that organization in Chapter 6.

Another way of stating all this is that proof is in the eye of the beholder. It's always strictly possible to say that this or that has not been proven. *But in most situations, including nonscientific ones, it is possible to accumulate sufficient evidence to yield a probability for a given result that most people would accept as "proof" and justification for action. Where that threshold occurs constantly comes up in scientific debates about things like evolution and global warming, and in court cases deciding guilt or innocence.*

> Hey, critical readers! Don't just take his word for it! Go bother your own scientist with the question.

So next time you hear someone going to the mat saying this thing has been proven or that other thing hasn't been proven, don't get distracted. Proof is in the eye of the beholder, which really just sort of reaffirms the whole risk-management idea. The useful question to ask about a scientific claim is not, Has this been proven? but, Is the evidence sufficient to yield a probability that justifies action in this case? In other words, given the risks involved, is this good enough to go on?

The lesson here is twofold. First, we need to learn to accept some haziness in scientific statements about what we know. Scientists are trained to not give absolute answers. It is interesting that in recent years, some have started to do so when talking with the media, because they've learned that whenever they include the very scientific words *possibly*, *perhaps*, and *uncertainty*, their conclusions are interpreted by the media and public as simple guesswork.

Second, scientific answers are usually very conservative, reporting only what is strongly defensible and confident. The full results are usually given as a range of possibilities, with confidence levels assigned to them (such as "we are 95 percent confident that the mean global surface temperature increased 1.33°F ± 0.32°F during the 100 years ending in 2005"). It's useful to keep in mind that what gets through the media machine to the lay person is usually something like "Temperatures rose 1.3°F last century." So such statements shouldn't be taken as "the answer."

Take-Home Tool: There is no use in waiting for something to be proven because, despite popular perception, science can never do that. And scientific statements are typically very conservative; researchers limit themselves to what they can say with a decent level of confidence.

There Is No (Such Thing as) Consensus

Sometimes you hear that there is no consensus among scientists about global warming.

It turns out there is no consensus among scientists on *any-thing*, at least in the common usage of the word to mean "every single person agrees." There will always be some scientist somewhere who disagrees. Why? Because, again, science is uncertain, which means there is simply no way to tell when you've discovered "reality." There is always room for disagreement, always an awareness that our understanding might be wrong.

Pick the most well-known, well-established scientific law you can think of. The law of gravity, right? Guess what? There's no *consensus* on it! We've got a satellite up there right now, *Gravity Probe B*, testing our current understanding of gravity. If you're waiting for there to be no dissent at all, then you'll wait forever, no matter what the scientific issue.

> Recently, there's even an alternative version of gravity being taken seriously, called modified Newtonian dynamics, if you're curious.

That's why you should try to avoid focusing on the word *consensus* in the global warming debate, because most people take that to mean "no one disagrees." So as soon as you can find a blog by a guy with a PhD saying, "I disagree," you think that there's no consensus and therefore the science is controversial and still in flux. Instead, use (or look for) terms like *well established, well understood, well accepted, overwhelming majority of scientific opinion, uncontroversial,* and *preponderance of opinion* because they describe a high level of confidence of what science knows, and statements that include these terms can survive the appearance of a dissenter. And there will always be dissenters in science on any issue.

> These are the standards that scientists themselves use as good enough to go on.

Take-Home Tool: The science will *never* be finished, and the existence of differing views doesn't disprove the claim that a scientific understanding is well established.

The Peer-Review Process

You do sometimes hear scientists use the word *consensus*. What they mean is that there is no longer significant debate in the scientific community. The way they make that judgment takes a practiced eye, but since you'll be wading back into the shouting match, it's worth developing a couple rules of thumb that will help in distinguishing what's controversial science from what's accepted science. It starts with understanding a little about how the scientific community debates ideas.

Because nothing can be proven, how do scientists tell good ideas from bad ones? Langenberg explains the way an idea is advanced: "Suppose I have an idea, a theory, or a new experimental result. I put it out for all my colleagues to see. Their task is to demonstrate that it has a flaw, that it's wrong in some sense, to undermine it if they can. If they can't, then my idea or result survives, and maybe I win a Nobel Prize."

Mr. Proof-Is-in-the-Eye-of-the-Beholder (see page 40).

My students have described this process of testing ideas in science as: "Hit it with a sledgehammer and see if it breaks. Whatever survives is the best we've got." Science is a very adversarial activity! Hence the old adage among physicists: Physics is a contact sport.

The formal part of this intellectual sledgehammering is called the *peer-review process.* If you want your scientific work to be taken seriously, you submit it as a paper to a peer-reviewed journal. These magazines send your article around to experts in that field, who try as hard as possible to poke holes in it, which you then have to fix before the journal will publish it. The greater the prestige of the journal, the harder it tries to break the submitted work, because the journal wants to protect its reputation by not publishing anything that later looks silly.

The stronger journals end up accepting only a small fraction of submitted papers. And because scientists can never claim to know The Truth, when a journal decides to publish a paper, it is not saying so much "This is correct" as it is saying, "The editors think this is worth looking at, and it might be important, and it's not obviously wrong." The overall collection of papers and articles that are published in peer-reviewed journals is what you'll hear referred to as "the [peer-reviewed] literature."

Over time, journals develop reputations among the scientific community. Because no scientist has the time to read all the published work in his or her field, a journal's reputation gives the individual a handy way to decide what's worth taking the time to read. For instance, the journals *Science, Nature, Physical Review Letters,* and *Proceedings of the National Academy of Sciences (PNAS)* are acknowledged to be top of the line, publishing only stuff that has stood up to severe pummeling.

Remember! Being published in a top journal doesn't mean it's true. Just that it's the best we've got.

In the shouting match, you'll hear things like "Show me a peer-reviewed article to back that up," and "Sure, that was peer reviewed, but it was in *Energy and the Environment,* which everyone knows is a bush-league journal." Scientists know which journals are respected, but we lay people are going to have to settle for knowing that peer-reviewed is more trustworthy than non peer-reviewed.

Take-Home Tool: In general, if a scientific claim hasn't been peer-reviewed, it's not worth too much. The exception is for very new claims, because the peer-review meat grinder turns slowly. In those cases, the reputation of the scientists involved provides a useful indication of whether the claim is worth considering.

Is It Getting Colder in Here, or Is It Just Me?

Have you ever felt frustrated at the whole name changing thing around global warming? First it was *global warming*, then it was *global climate change* (or, if you are a science buff, *anthropogenic climate change*), and now we're starting to hear the terms *climate disruption* and *climate destabilization*. This gives the impression that the lab coats are just making stuff up as they go along.

> C'mon, Dr. Warmingstein— which is it?

It's just like that global cooling scare in the 1970s, when magazines splashed warnings on their covers about the impending ice age. Why the heck should we listen to the climate geeks now, if just a few years ago they were saying something totally opposite? Doesn't that mean that we can expect them to change their minds again in another few years, maybe this time saying "Oops! We were mistaken. Sorry for scaring you into ruining your economy and throwing away your freedoms. Our bad."

The answer is, yes, the eggheads *are* always changing their minds. But—and here's the critical point—it's always in favor of the better idea. A perfect example is that global cooling scare. It was a bit like a murder detective talking to the press in the early stages of an investigation. He's got lots of different possible explanations for what happened, and the media grabs the most salacious one to trumpet all over the place. So when the detective later presents a different version, the public thinks the fuzz are just groping around, when in fact the later idea is the much more solid one.

If you dig around and look at what the scientific community itself (and not the media) was saying in the '70s, it was essentially "Hey, the climate seems much more unstable than

> Because it's survived the sledgehammer assault that global cooling did not.

we'd thought. It's even possible that an ice age could appear within the next hundred years." It was that last bit that got splashed around in the media. So now, what looks on the face of it to be a total reversal—the globe is warming—is really just a narrowing down of the possibilities and is likely to be much more confident than any previous pronouncements.

As time progresses, the statements from science tend to get closer and closer to the truth, but they never actually claim to get there.

Take-Home Tool: The answer to the question, The brainiacs keep contradicting what they said before, so why should I listen to them now? is, Because the new answer is more solid than the old one. It's not perfect, and it will never be certain. But it is, literally, the best we've got because science will never claim to know The Truth.

Who's Your Authority Figure, Huh, Punk?

In science, ideas ultimately have to stand on their own. But that takes a long time to be demonstrated. In the meantime, the peer-review process sorts out the kooky and sloppy stuff, and the relative prestige of the journals provides a handy tool for the

> Gravity's still up for debate, remember?

working scientist to prioritize which ideas to take seriously for the moment. An additional way for getting a quick sense of the merit of an idea is to look at the authorities behind it.

A lot of us have a knee-jerk reaction to not trust authority. But in science, authority is a useful rule of thumb for how solid the ideas of that person (or institution, such as a journal or an organization) is likely to be. Sort of like the way a winning racehorse has more authority, not because someone gave it to it but because of its successful track record.

In science, you get to be an authority by, well, a lot of people thinking you are an authority. That happens if you get a lot of quality stuff through the peer-review process and—here's a key point—people *cite* your work, using the findings from your studies as *givens* in their own work. That is your track record. If Ricky and Lucy both get work published in peer-reviewed journals, but way more people are citing Lucy's work than Ricky's, that's a pretty good indication that people are giving her the greater authority, and in a blind bet, they would bet on Lucy's ideas.

Poor Ricky. Work smarter, not harder, Ricky!

Take-Home Tool: At the end of the day, ideas in science do need to stand on their own. But in the middle of the day, authority is a useful predictor when placing bets. It's not conclusive, but it's how science in the real world works, and again, it's the best we've got.

But I Might Be Wrong

One of my students proposed the most succinct and insightful definition of science that I've come across: "Science is the observation of errors." It's got the whole nature of science in there: the basis in empirical observations; the sledgehammer test; the built-in uncertainty; and the self-critical, self-correcting attitude. As much as we think science is about being right, the actual practice of the stuff is largely focused on being wrong.

Extra credit for Zach!

Why? Because being open to the possibility that you might be wrong is exactly how you get *less* wrong over time, sort of like saying "I'd better find all the holes in my argument before someone else can." Strangely, the way to make your ideas stronger is to try to break them. Looking for errors in your understanding rather than just trying to find supporting evidence is the best way to improve your ideas.

The sledgehammer again! Preemptively self-inflicted?

This is useful for the lay person as well. Each of us is right now walking around with some mistaken understandings. If we don't admit that possibility, then we lose the opportunity to get rid of those mistaken understandings and replace them with some that are closer to the truth before the mistakes do us harm (or humiliate us, as is most often the case for me).

Science is all about trying to align our understanding more closely with physical reality, which requires a good bit of uncomfortable humility. I would suggest that in the shouting match about global warming, your goal should be somewhat similar. After all, when you fall out a 10th-story window, gravity doesn't care about what you *believe* will happen. That is why, religion aside, it is fundamentally in your own best interest to change your beliefs to fit how the physical world works rather than hoping that it's the other way around.

This can be quite challenging to the ego, but it is simply pragmatic. When it comes to something as all-encompassing as the climate—which influences every part of human activity—I've come

What!? I might be wrong?

to realize that being humble about my understanding makes it less likely for the laws of physics to end up spanking me hard. I'd much rather admit I might be wrong than have the physical world demonstrate the point to me unequivocally and painfully.

Take-Home Tool: Always keep in mind that it is in your own best interest to ask yourself, Could I be wrong? Because that's how you move your understanding closer to physical reality and then make good decisions—that is, ones that are more likely to bring you happiness and security.

Assumptions Training
(Hup, Hup, Hup . . .)

Perhaps the greatest source of mistakes is unknowingly making assumptions that don't turn out to be true. That's why scientists are explicitly trained in rooting those out from their own work and why they tend to be very cautious in any statements they make. They've been humbled by experience as well as specifically trained to not get too cocky.

> Like Langenberg prefacing his statement quoted on page 40.

This rooting out of assumptions is a tremendously powerful tool to help avoid shooting yourself in the foot by going full throttle with a mistaken understanding. I think it will be especially useful as you choose your bet on the climate change issue. So let's give you a chance to do a little training.

Audience participation time. Get an index card and use it to force yourself to read the following questions only one line at a time and to keep your eyes from darting ahead to the answers.

> This book may seem to be about global warming but really it's about thinking tools applied to global warming.

I'm going to use examples other than global warming, because they are much more commonly accessible to the non–climate geek. We'll start with some classic riddles and then move on to other examples.

If you'd like, try to solve the riddle before looking at the answer. But the real exercise comes after that: Once you know the answer, try to identify the common assumption people unknowingly make that results in making the riddle hard to solve. I can vouch from personal experience that practicing looking for my unconscious assumptions has made it much easier to identify them in my daily life and has been very useful.

For instance, when I'm in a discussion with someone, and we just seem to be talking past each other, I try to identify what assumptions I have been making. This often leads to a realization of why we're not hearing each other, and I can change my approach to something much less frustrating for both of us.

Okay, here are the exercises. Get your index card in position:

Q: A man going to bed flips off the light switch, yet still manages to get into his bed across the room before it's dark. How did he manage this?

A: He went to bed during daylight hours. What was the assumption that kept this answer from being immediately clear? Try to figure this out before reading the next line.

Assume no superpowers.

Assumption: *He went to bed at night (at a time and latitude such that it is dark outside).*

Q: 1 + 1 = 10. What's wrong with this statement?

A: Nothing. If you use base-two math, that is. (That's the whole zeros and ones thing that computers are based on.) What was the assumption?

Assumption: *That I was using the typical base-10 math. An interesting note here is that if others see the equation and think I'm a dope for making such an error, it turns out that they are the ones making the error, even as they point their finger at me. This example is tricky, yes. But when you think the person you're talking to doesn't get it, there is always the possibility that you are the one who is mistaken, and it's worth stopping to double-check your thinking.*

Q: You already know that I'm nervous about potentially difficult times ahead from dangerous climate change. When I tried to shift my retirement investments into a more conservative posture because of that, the broker thought I was just spooked by the market (this was before the financial upheaval of late 2008) and tried to talk me out of it, saying that downturns always cor-

rect themselves. We talked past each other for a while and it got frustrating for both of us. After I hung up the phone, I realized it was because we each held different assumptions about investments. Can you guess what they were?

Assumption: *He assumes that the next 30 years will look pretty much like the last 30, and I don't. If I had realized that at the time, I could have mentioned it and saved us both a bit of headache.*

Q: Here's one I use in my classroom. I tell the students that we're going to get creamed in Friday night's football game because—have they heard?—the opposing side's offensive line has an average weight of over 340 pounds! That usually worries them, until I tell them that the linemen weigh 110, 103, 98, 97, and 1,296 pounds. What was the assumption that caused the worry?

Assumption: *Most of us make the unconscious assumption that most things in a group are fairly close to the average. This is why I don't feel qualified to evaluate the significance of statements such as "global mean temperatures have not significantly increased statistically since 1998" that you'll hear in the shouting match. It may be a true statement—just like my statement about the average weight of the linemen—but I know that I can be easily fooled by seemingly simple numbers, so I try not to bet too much on them.*

Here's one of my absolute favorite mind-blower activities.

> You can stop reading with the index card now.

Hold this book about 18 inches in front of your face. Now close your left eye, and with your right eye focus on the *X* on the next page. Keep your eye focused on the *X*, but pay attention to the dot as you slowly move the book toward your face.

Did you see it??! Did you see the dot disappear? Bizarre,

huh? That's called your blind spot, and it's due to the way your retina is put together. But the totally amazing thing that blows me away every time is—you didn't even know you had it! Unlike a car's blind spot, which you can check because you know it's there, with this blind spot *you don't even know to go looking.* You simply don't see anything there—not even the absence of anything! Your brain doesn't even recognize that there's a "there" there in which you might see something.

It really makes you wonder what else might be going on like that, not with your eyesight but *with your mind,* with your understanding of the world. Kinda creepy, huh?

Okay, one more.

This one depends on your timing, so follow the instructions carefully to get it right. Go get a pen and paper now. Back yet?

Do not turn the page until I tell you to. On page 54, there is a simple illustration. When I say go, what you're going to do is turn the page, glance at the illustration for just half a second and then turn back here for further instructions. Got it?

Okay. Ready, set, *go.*

Now that you've glanced at the illustration, make a brief sketch on your paper of what you saw. Do that now.

And now turn the page and look at the illustration again.

Did you do it correctly? Because you've been training your awareness during this chapter (or, rather, getting more suspicious of my tricks), you may very well have. But it probably wouldn't surprise you to know that most people incorrectly write "Paris in the spring" instead of the correct "Paris in the the spring" (with two *the*'s).

I gave this example last because it ties together a couple of things. The first is that we make assumptions based on our past experiences. We assume our future experiences will be similar to our past experiences, like the broker's assumption that the market will bounce back soon because in his 30-year experience, it always has. (In the "the" example, the past experience is reading grammatically correct sentences.)

And the other thing is that such assumptions are not necessarily a bad thing! We make assumptions because it allows our brains to fill in the blanks quickly when we don't have the time or opportunity to completely figure out the picture at hand. This type of filling in the blanks is why it deosn't mttaer in waht oredr the ltteers in a wrod are, the olny iprmoatnt tihng is taht the frist and lsat ltteer be in the rghit pclaes.

"The last 20 saber-toothed tigers tried to eat me. I wonder if this one will be my friend," doesn't work out so well.

So assumptions are not necessarily bad. The problem arises when you make them *without knowing it* because it leads to the deceptive thought that things are simple when in fact they may be very complex. This is the danger of listening to the shouting match without first having some tools or filters in place. There are arguments on both sides that, although they sound reasonable and quite straightforward, rely on incorrect assumptions and so provide an answer that is probably wrong. That is why scientists are explicitly trained in eliminating assumptions from their work and why the greatest wisdom is to know that you do not know.

Take-Home Tool: It is in your own best interest to look for your unconscious assumptions when you dive into a complex or emotional issue. Think of how unsettling that blind-spot activity was, and then ask yourself: "Could I be holding an as-

PARIS
IN THE
THE SPRING

sumption about the global warming debate that I don't even realize I have?"

A Word Against Common Sense

As long as I'm ticking people off by pointing out how easily fooled we all are, I might as well take on that sacred cow common sense.

The problem with common sense is that it fools us into thinking we understand when we may not. It is built on unconscious assumptions that may or may not be valid, but we'll never know. It gives false confidence when we are best served by humility. And it lulls us into stopping when we should dig deeper. So, it often leads us to a wrong conclusion.

> How can you check something you don't even realize you have?

- It is common sense that the earth is flat. Just look at it!

- It is common sense that the sun circles the earth instead of the other way around. Try it. Point to the sun, and then a few hours later do it again. Your arm moved! And the earth is right where you left it. (Clearly it's too big to have gone anywhere.)

- It is common sense that tiny amounts of something can't affect a huge system. (Try living without the magnesium that makes up only 0.05 percent of your body. *Hint*: You can't.)

Common sense, like assumptions, can be very helpful as a shortcut when time is short and the stakes are low. But it is too easily fooled to be trusted for decisions about complex topics with high stakes.

In this book, as I try to simplify the very complex topic of global warming, I'm sure I will end up demonstrating how easy it is for errors to creep in. If you catch an error or get frustrated with my oversimplifications, then ask yourself: Isn't that exactly what your common sense does—boil down the complex to the oversimplified and then render judgment?

Take-Home Tool: Remember not to be a slave to common sense. In a complex world, common sense makes for a useful suggestion but a lousy conclusion.

The Equipment So Far

Before we move on to the next set of tools for approaching the shouting match, it's worth listing what we've got so far. Useful tools that come from understanding the nature of science:

- There's no use in waiting for something to be proven.
- Scientific statements are usually very conservative, limited to only what scientists can say with high confidence (or with an explicitly stated level of confidence).
- There's no use in waiting for the science to be settled, and the presence of differing views doesn't mean that something is controversial.
- Peer-reviewed papers are the basic currency in science.
- Scientists who change their minds are not waffling but are progressing toward a better understanding of reality.
- Although science is indeed all about pursuing the truth, it never claims to actually get there.
- Authority in science is a valid thing to consider, though it doesn't mean the authority is right.
- Asking yourself if you could be wrong is uncomfortable and difficult, but it's in your own practical interest.
- Asking yourself about the assumptions you bring to any issue is also very useful in improving your odds for making a decision you'll be happy with.
- Relying on common sense for a complex topic is not generally useful.

Understanding a bit about how science works will go a long way in making sense of the shouting match as you go about creating your own decision grid. Now that we've explored the nature of science, let's do the same for that other big factor in the debate: your brain.

CHAPTER 3

OUR GLITCHY BRAINS: "HAVE I BEEN A FOOL? OH, LET ME COUNT THE WAYS!"

I'm sorry, but you've got a defective brain. Don't feel bad—we've all got one. It's standard issue. But the key to dealing with the pitfalls of our very human brains is to know where those pitfalls are so that we can avoid them more often. That's what we'll explore in this chapter so that you can be on your guard against yourself when entering the shouting match in your search for information for building your decision grid.

And there's a strict no-exchange policy. I've checked.

In the last chapter, we saw how unconscious assumptions can lead you astray. But the first brain glitch we'll explore here is an even more devilish malfunction because, unlike assumptions that trip you up when you're *not* looking, this one trips you up when you *are* looking.

Confirmation Bias

In 1960, psychologist Peter Wason ran an experiment in which a researcher would show volunteer subjects a trio of numbers (say, 2, 4, 6) and tell them that the trio fit a particular rule. The volunteers' task was to guess the rule by coming up with their own trios and asking the researcher if they fit the rule. The participants could do this as many times as they wanted until they were sure they had figured out what the rule was; then they would tell it to the researcher.

The rule was simply "any ascending sequence," but the volunteers had a heck of a time discovering that. They would instead come up with rules that were way more complicated than necessary. Why?

The reason is that the volunteers tended to test only trios that fit a rule they tentatively had in mind to begin with; in other words, they tried to *confirm* that they had come up with the right rule. What they did not do was try to challenge their rule by testing trios that did *not* fit. In techno-jargon, they did not attempt to falsify their hypothesis. So they got lots of confirmation for their idea, but ended up with an incorrect conclusion. This seems backward: Usually we assume that if you find lots of confirmation for an idea, then that idea must be pretty close to the truth.

This fun phenomenon was dubbed *confirmation bias* and is an intrinsic part of the psychology of human brains. In fact, I've come to think that it is at the center of the deadlock in the popular debate over climate change, for which we have so bloody much information but can't seem to agree on what action is in our best interest.

But how on earth could attempting to falsify your hypothesis lead to a better understanding of what's going on? Allow me to illustrate with my dog.

Here? Here? Here?

Louie is lovable but a bit of a doofus. (As a puppy he actually managed to get stuck sitting on his own head. Twice.) He'll yelp at the slightest goosing. One morning as he started to get up, he yelped and sank back down. I watched, and this happened a couple times. I was very concerned, especially since I've known a couple of dogs who had suddenly surfacing spinal tumors, and Louie clearly wasn't able to get up due to paralyzing pain. So I started gently poking and prodding over his entire body, trying to find what hurt by paying attention to his occasional yelps. I eventually decided that something was definitely going on between his shoulder blades.

Hi guys! What's up? Are we gonna go outside?

I went downstairs to discuss the next steps with my wife and turned around to see Doofus trotting after me. Over the next day, the yelps went away completely, and he's fine now. We still don't know what was wrong. But it's pretty clear it wasn't a spinal tumor between his shoulder blades. So how did I end up being convinced something was going on in that specific spot?

Let's assume Louie yelps at random times during the poking and prodding. When I hear a yelp, I take that as a sign that I'm in the right general area, so I limit the prodding to that area. Another yelp tells me I'm warmer, so I focus on that even smaller section. And so on. Eventually, I'm probing around just a couple inches for several minutes, and when the next yelp comes, that confirms that I've found the exact spot!

> Like we saw in Chapter 2, this is why the peer-review process in science is so important. Others who wouldn't share your particular bias check to see if your procedure is susceptible to confirmation bias.

So using my very objective and careful method, the dog's random yelping would lead me to be just as confident in my conclusion as I would have been if he were really hurting somewhere.

I would have gotten a result that was closer to reality (that he was just being a lovable dork who likes to be touched) if I had probed areas *other* than what I suspected. For instance, if I thought the problem was between his shoulder blades, I should have monkeyed around with his foot for a bit.

> That is, to attempt to falsify my hypothesis.

If he doesn't yelp (that is, I failed to falsify my hypothesis), then I come away more confident that my suspicion of his shoulder blades is a decent one. If he does yelp during the foot massage (that is, I falsified my hypothesis), then I realize that the shoulder blades aren't such a great guess after all. Either way, trying to falsify my hypothesis improves my understanding of what's really going on.

> Can we just say "contradict my belief" from now on?

This is sort of like the sledgehammer

I try to **falsify** my idea that there's a problem between Louie's shoulder blades by massaging his foot.

 SILENCE

YELP!

He remains quiet as I massage his foot. **Hypothesis not falsified.**

He yelps as I massage his foot. **Hypothesis falsified!**

I'm **more confident** in my hypothesis that the problem is between his shoulder blades.

Now I know it was a bad hypothesis and I need to **change it** if I want to figure out what's going on.

Either way, I win!

Trying to falsify your hypothesis is a win-win.

view that my students came up with. One way to make your idea more robust is to actively seek to break it. If it breaks, then you know it wasn't a decent idea; that's a good thing to be aware of so that you can either fix it or get rid of it. And if it survives all the sledgehammering, then you come out with increased confidence. Either way, you win—you end up better off.

Page 43.

Although being left with shattered idea bits all over the floor can indeed be a bit of a downer. I had a student who shattered a beautiful idea that I'd been building up successfully for years, and we've been unable to put it back together. Thanks a lot, Stacy.

A Smorgasbord of Flavors

As we've discussed, the simplest form of confirmation bias is seeking to confirm your ideas while never checking to see if you can contradict them. But confirmation bias shows up in many other ways, and to guard against it, you will be well served by being able to recognize all its wily incarnations.

One flavor of confirmation bias is known as counting the hits but not the misses. Like when you're thinking of a friend, and then she calls you at that moment and you think, "Wow, that was weird. Maybe I'm psychic." You count that as a hit. But you haven't counted all the times that you've thought of a friend and she hasn't immediately called (all the misses).

This is sometimes referred to as the That Van Is Always on the Corner syndrome. It seems like every time you pass that corner, you see the same van and thus think there is something suspicious going on. In reality, you've passed that corner a million times when it's empty, but the empty corner never draws your attention, so you don't end up counting the misses. The result is, every time you look at that corner, the van is indeed there (because those were the only times you "looked").

One way this shows up in the global warming debate is when you see headlines that agree with what you are already inclined to think: You tend to read those articles ("Aha! See— more evidence that I'm right!") and skip the articles with headlines that contradict your belief. So you come away with an impression that the balance of evidence is in your favor.

Another flavor of confirmation bias is when you look at all the evidence (for and against your position) but then tend to give more weight to the bits that *support* your view and less to those that contradict it. This leads to what's called *belief polarization*, and it pretty much explains political discourse (as well as the popular debate over global warming). Everyone is looking at the same pile of evidence, and everyone thinks the pile supports his or her own belief while disproving opposing views.

Let's face it. We all want to be right. When we sift through a pile of evidence, what are we looking for? Stuff to support our view, of course. So that's what gets picked up. It's like sticking a magnet in a bucket of iron filings and black sand: the magnet is tuned only to the filings, and that's all that sticks. So you pull the magnet out and go away thinking: "That's a bucket of iron filings."

In a sense, this isn't really news to most of us. We're all familiar with the expressions "You tend to see what you want to see" and "When you have a hammer, everything looks like a nail." But if you're anything like me, once you start watching for confirmation bias, you'll see it in yourself all the time.

Murphy's Law of Research expresses confirmation bias in another way: If you do enough research, you can find support for your theory. With so much information out there, the popular debate over global warming is particularly prone to this. Indeed, with Google at your fingertips, you can find supporting evidence for pretty much any belief you care to try. I'm serious! Do a bit of searching about the geocentric theory—the idea that the sun goes around the earth—and you'll find arguments that you won't be able to counter without resorting to some version of "But everyone knows most scientists say otherwise!"

Some of the Many Flavors of Confirmation Bias

- **Confirmation bias proper:** *Looking for evidence* to confirm your beliefs but never seeking out evidence to contradict them.

- **Counting the hits but not the misses:** *Paying attention* only when an event confirms your belief. Also known as That Van Is Always on the Corner.

- **Belief polarization:** *Giving more credibility* to evidence that fits your ideas and less to evidence that contradicts them.

- **Murphy's Law of Research:** *Enough research* will reveal evidence to confirm any hypothesis.

Craven Is a Fool

Confirmation bias is not simply misleading, it is something far, far worse. I want to illustrate how insidious confirmation bias is by ridiculing myself. I do this to emphasize how powerful and universal this brain glitch is and how watchful you should be for your own hiccups, because no one is immune. I spend my career explicitly teaching about confirmation bias, and I *still* fall for it again and again, with sometimes painful results.

I know others are going to do it, so I might as well get a head start.

A couple years ago, as part of a spectacular air-guitar leap off a desk during a triumphant routine for my high school's lip-synch contest (teachers rule!), I landed on my ankle wrong. Hard. I iced it that night and then proceeded about my life, limping around the halls of school. It wasn't until six months later—after I finally got X-rays and an MRI taken because it still hurt—that I learned I had broken it.

Due to my pigheadedness (that is, confirmation bias), the whole time I paid attention only to the signs that indicated a bad sprain (I could still walk) and ignored any signs telling me it might be broken (I could only barely walk, despite my high pain tolerance). As a result of that particularly nasty episode of confirmation bias, I'm stuck saying "old lip-synch injury" when the ankle acts up, which sounds way less cool than "old football injury." (Not to mention way more ridiculous.)

My point is, ain't none of us immune from confirmation bias—ever. The best we can do is try to be aware of it, particularly in situations in which the consequences might be significant. It is no shame to admit you might be falling prey to it in any situation. In fact, it is in your best interests to do so.

This brings me to a flavor of confirmation bias that I've fallen for so often that I'm going to name it after myself:

> **The Craven Principle: You're probably not as smart as you think you are. And that can bite you big-time.**

When I shared the Craven Principle with my wife, she was not so convinced that I had discovered a keen insight into human nature. ("Well, duh," I think were her words.) But I think the more tools you possess to help you watch for this stealthy opponent, the more likely you are to avoid it.

The Real Enemy

Why am I making such a big deal about confirmation bias? If it were merely another bump in the road to understanding, I wouldn't devote most of a chapter to it. But it is a critical obstacle due to one factor: It makes us overconfident.

Confirmation bias doesn't just trick you into being wrong. It tricks you into being wrong *with confidence*. So you end up placing a much higher wager on the bet than is really wise. And you don't even realize it until you lose. That's the terribly deceptive nature of overconfidence: By definition, you don't know you are overconfident until it's too late, and you are so confident that it never even occurs to you to have a plan B.

Confirmation bias takes your understanding further from physical reality, precisely when you think you are getting *closer* to it because you are doing careful research. Confirmation bias is worse than a thief who just takes your money. It's a con man who tricks you into happily volunteering your money because you think you're getting a great deal—and you thank him for it! What a shyster!

That's why I've come to regard confirmation bias as the

real enemy in this debate, despite having the very convenient scapegoat of people who disagree with me. I've got this onboard con man in my brain, and so do those who disagree with me, and between us is a mountain of evidence just ripe for belief polarization. So we end up locked in an epic stalemate, even though there is plenty of evidence for making reasonable judgments about the probabilities and risks of global warming.

Just Like Lima Beans

Although the real con man is in your brain, it is also probably being encouraged by people in the world. So who is it that's trying to dupe you in this global warming shouting match? Liberal elites? Corporate CEOs? The scientific establishment? The economic establishment? The United Nations? Big Oil? I'm not smart enough and I haven't done enough research to feel comfortable leveling such weighty accusations. But I do suggest that it's in your best interest to lift your head up from the shell game for a second and say, "Heeeeyyy—wait a minute . . . !"

Confirmation bias can be so stealthy that learning to be vigilant of it by questioning yourself is critical, especially when dealing with a contentious issue like climate change. It is extremely unpleasant, yes, but it is simply in your best interests. Just like eating lima beans.

I know that I've become a lot less righteous than I used to be because of the ridiculous number of times I've confidently shot myself in the foot. Realizing how unlikely it is for me to always be right—and how powerful confirmation bias is—I've learned to constantly check over my shoulder for that gremlin. And I think I probably make better decisions as a result.

Knowing how to combat your own confirmation bias helps remove that huge handicap that we all share—the tendency for our beliefs to drift toward what we *want* to be true. When the wager may be the whole ball of wax, that's probably not the best way to decide where to place your bet.

> The global economy in the top left of the grid on global warming, or the global climate in the bottom right.

Immunizing Yourself Against Yourself

So now that you fear your own brain, what can you do to domesticate it? As with all problems, the first step is admitting you have one. This really is the hardest part. One online exchange that I'll always remember as a cautionary tale was with someone who wrote a lengthy and hostile critique of my videos, arguing that global warming was a hoax. I wrote back, "What if you're wrong?" His response was an expansion of his original points, and I responded by pointing out that he hadn't addressed my question, asking him again, "What if you're wrong?" His response?

"I'm not wrong."

How much further do you think that conversation got? This person was not stupid or evil or deficient. He was just human, with the same glitchy brain and the same hungry ego as the rest of us. It is a universal human affliction, I'm afraid. The best we can do is try to limit the trouble our defective brains cause us.

You know how you have little red flags that sometimes go up in your head to warn you that something might be going on and you should pay closer attention? What I've found most useful in combating my confirmation bias is to install some additional red flags in my brain, ones that are tripped by clues that my bias might be in operation. When a red flag goes up, it doesn't mean I'm wrong. It's just a reminder to step a little more deliberately through the landscape I'm currently exploring because it may have some traps set by my brain.

The higher the stakes, the greater care you probably want

to take in forming your opinion, and having an alarm set up to warn you that you're on fertile ground for confirmation bias will make you happier with your results. So here are some red flags that might be useful to you. They indicate that it's worth pausing and asking yourself, "Am I being as foolish as Craven?"

RED FLAG 1: You catch yourself looking only for evidence to support your view rather than evidence to contradict it. Of course, when you are trying to make a careful decision, you need to see that there are good points supporting your view. But remember that you need to spend at least some time actively looking for things that contradict it. Think of it this way: When you come across something you disagree with, you typically go looking for something to disprove it. But when you come across something you do agree with, you *don't* try to disprove it. So guess which type of thing you'll end up disproving more often?

RED FLAG 2: You find yourself thinking, Why can't they see? It's so obvious! Classic belief polarization—they can't see because even though they are looking at the same pile of evidence you are, they are choosing to give weight to different bits. It's most likely the other guy who is letting his confirmation bias interfere with his judgment (because you're probably the one who's right, right?). But there is always the uncomfortable possibility that it is you.

RED FLAG 3: You really, really hope something is true. The stronger our desire for something to be true, the more susceptible we are to confirmation bias. This is why comforting messages are more dangerous than alarming ones. We really want things to be okay. So we'll tend to listen to things that confirm that assessment more than things that contradict it. Again, that doesn't mean that your understanding is incorrect. But it is worth examining such assurances more closely than you feel inclined to because they are ripe for confirmation bias.

RED FLAG 4: You stop investigating once you find an answer you agree with. Remember Murphy's Law of Research.

RED FLAG 5: You find yourself doing a little touchdown dance. You may even chant, "See! I was right! I was right!" A version of red flag 4.

Page 63.

RED FLAG 6: You find yourself thinking, That guy just isn't making any sense. I came up with this one after I fell for it. I'd been having an extensive debate by email with someone who held an opposing view. Fairly far into the back and forth, I was trying to make sense of a long response of his, but I just couldn't do it. I reread and reread and was befuddled, thinking, "He's all over the place—I just don't know how to respond to this." And then I thought, "Ahh, maybe that's a clue to examine my own thinking. Maybe he's being perfectly clear, and I don't know how to respond because *he's right* but I just won't let myself see that." It's useful to be willing to take a step back and ask, "Could I be the one who's wrong here?"

RED FLAG 7: You are very confident of your views. Okay, this one is a total catch-22, but it's worth being aware of it. The Dunning-Kruger effect is the tendency for people to be *less* confident of their views as they gain *more* skill and knowledge. The flip side is that those with the least knowledge tend to be the most confident. It's counterintuitive—that greater knowledge leads to less confidence—but it fits well with the

No joke—it's an established psychological phenomenon.

Our Glitchy Brains: "Have I Been a Fool? Oh, Let Me Count the Ways!"

old adage "The greatest wisdom is to know that you do not know."

🏃 **RED FLAG 8: You can't come up with a reasonable answer to the question, What would it take to change my views?** This is a pretty good indicator that your onboard con man is doubling as a bouncer, making sure that there is no way any contradictory evidence will ever get in to violate your cherished view. You may indeed be right, but if you're not, you won't know until it's too late.

🏃 **RED FLAG 9: You think you've found a knockout blow.** It's entirely possible. But given the self-deceptive power of the brain, it's a high-stakes bet. If you veto all other arguments because of a single knockout blow, then you're essentially betting your entire opinion on your confidence that you are not being influenced by confirmation bias about that one argument. I've learned to be wary of giving a single statement veto power over everything else. I've been human (that is, mistaken) just too many times.

🏃 **RED FLAG 10: When someone is challenging your decision, you eventually hear yourself saying, "I just think . . ."** This is often the last refuge of someone who has run out of good arguments but is still unwilling to let go of his current opinion. Remember, your quest is not to hold on to your opinion but to make a decision that is the most likely to best serve your interests.

🏃 **RED FLAG 11: You feel indignant or righteous.** Pride can be a real drag sometimes. I once walked for hours though empty streets in the middle of the night in a city in India because I refused the outrageous price demanded by the only autorickshaw driver around. I could easily afford the price; I just didn't want him to win. My feet ended up literally sore from that particular instance of shooting them. Sometimes indignation is indeed appropriate. I'm just saying to check.

Actions

Once you're tipped off that your confirmation bias may be in play, how do you combat it? The good news is 90 percent of the solution is simply being aware of the problem, because the con man relies on you not noticing the con that he's trying to pull. So just having those red flags installed in your brain will neutralize your confirmation bias most of the time.

Other things you can do when tipped off:

- Back up and start over. Try to pretend that you don't have an opinion yet and reexamine whatever you were looking at that triggered the red flag.
- Ask yourself, "Could I be wrong?" Then devote a couple minutes to visualizing what it would look and feel like to realize you're wrong and admit it. Then reexamine the trigger.
- Think about past times when you were confident but turned out to be wrong. Then reexamine the trigger.
- Go deliberately searching for evidence or arguments that would contradict your opinion. Recognize that the end point of your evaluation is not "feeling right" but "searching for contradictory evidence and not finding much."
- If it was a comforting message that triggered your confirmation bias, think through what the scenario would be if that comforting message turned out to be wrong. Come up with a plan B for that event.
- Make a list of things that—if you saw them—would change your mind.

> Like you did at the start of Chapter 1.

Other Problems with Our Brains

While confirmation bias is the main con man in the game, another feature of our human psychology may play a significant role in the global warming debate.

A couple years back, an editor from the *Los Angeles Times* contacted Harvard psychologist Daniel Gilbert with a question. Gilbert is a bestselling author about how the mind works, and the editor wanted to know why people weren't more worked up about global warming, since it was a potentially devastating threat. "And don't tell me that people just don't care about the future," wrote the editor, "because people do all sorts of things with the future in mind, such as quitting smoking and saving for retirement. But for some reason they don't seem to get bent out of shape over global warming. What can psychology tell us about that?"

As an answer, Gilbert wrote an essay in the *Los Angeles Times* titled "If Only Gay Sex Caused Global Warming." His basic point was that the human brain's alarm system has been conditioned over time to respond to threats that are immediate and visible. And it does an excellent job at that. But global climate change is a complete mismatch for our defenses because it has none of the features that our threat-alert system is tuned to. Gilbert proposes that we are conditioned to respond most strongly to threats that:

Call it the saber-toothed tiger reflex, if you want.

- **Are intentional and personal.** "Global warming isn't trying to kill us, and that's a shame. If climate change had been visited on us by a brutal dictator or an evil empire, the war on warming would be this nation's top priority."

- **Violate our moral sensibilities.** "Yes, global warming is bad, but it doesn't make us feel nauseated or angry or disgraced, and thus we don't feel compelled to rail against it as we do against other momentous threats to our species. . . . The fact is that if climate change were caused by gay sex, or by the practice of eating kittens, millions of protesters would be massing in the streets."

- **Are a clear and present danger.** "The brain is a beautifully engineered get-out-of-the-way machine that constantly scans the environment for things out of whose way it should right now get. That's what brains did for several hundred million years. . . . The application that allows us to respond to visible baseballs is ancient and reliable, but the add-on utility that allows us to respond to threats that loom in an unseen future is still in beta testing."

- **Involve quick changes rather than gradual changes.** "The density of Los Angeles traffic has increased dramatically in the last few decades, and citizens have tolerated it with only the obligatory grumbling. Had that change happened on a single day last summer, Angelenos would have shut down the city, called in the National Guard and lynched every politician they could get their hands on."

Global warming has none of these properties. It is impersonal, morally neutral, in the future, and gradual, and we're just not wired to watch out for stuff like that. So our level of concern as a society doesn't match the magnitude of what is being threatened by some of the scientists.

I sometimes just ask people what they think about this whole global warming thing and listen to their answers without betraying any of my own biases. One evening, I got a valuable insight into our wily brains from a local gas station attendant. This woman's answer was fairly typical of what I hear—it's probably a problem, but won't happen for a long time, so we shouldn't get too worked up about it—but her summary line really stuck with me. She said with a laugh, "If it were time to panic, it would be too late."

I've thought a lot about that line because I sense there's a deep insight there into how our brains work, but I can't quite put my finger on it. Surely it ties into what Gilbert writes. But there's something more. I find myself thinking, Does that mean there is no way to prevent a panic-worthy situation? Must we be panicked before we can work to solve the thing that's panicking us? Does that mean—even if global warming isn't a problem—that we are ultimately doomed anyway, because unless a threat triggers our saber-toothed tiger reflex, we will never act until it's too late?

I still can't put my finger on it. If you think you've got the answer, please tell me at www.gregcraven.org. I certainly don't have all the answers. But that line continues to haunt me.

Eat Your Lima Beans

As humans, we reflexively reject arguments that contradict what we would like to be true. We can't get rid of that reflex (standard-issue brain, and all), but we can perhaps redirect it to better serve us. I suggest that each of us would end up better off if we trained that reflex to trigger a closer examination of our beliefs. I'm proposing that converting the reflex from "reject this statement" to "watch for confirmation bias" is simply a pragmatic thing to do, because as we choose which lottery ticket in the global warming grid is a better bet, we are placing a wager about how the physical world works. In any disagreement between what we want to be true and what *is* true, physical reality wins every time. To narrow any gap, it's got to be the beliefs that do the moving. So it is simply pragmatic to be as open as you can to doing just that, to increase the chance that you place a winning bet.

Although it is extremely difficult and tiring (not to mention annoying) to constantly watch for my own confirmation bias, I do it because I want to end up with the most robust, solid viewpoint I can, so that I don't find myself holding on to something flimsy just because I really like the idea or really dislike the alternative—especially when I may be betting my family's future on the outcome. We simply cannot afford to give climate change anything but the most careful, most deliberate, most self-critical evaluation of our lives.

How silly would it be to end up in either of the disaster boxes in the grid (foolish action or foolish nonaction) and realize you'd spent more time putting together your fantasy football teams than analyzing the climate change debate?

CHAPTER 4

A BEAUTIFUL RAINBOW OF CREDIBILITY: THE CREDIBILITY SPECTRUM

I am not qualified to perform surgery on my kid, formulate my painkillers, fix my transmission, or analyze the intricacies of climate science (the most complex science in the history of, well, science). So unless I want to go out and earn a whole slew of PhDs, I'm simply going to have to listen to what experts say about important things.

As you saw in the last two chapters, the big danger of doing that with a complex scientific topic is that it plays right to a bunch of weak points in our brains: confirmation bias, unconscious assumptions, common sense, and so on. This chapter presents a tool I developed to combat those weaknesses in myself. I've found it tremendously powerful because it helps me keep my eye on the prize (estimating probabilities and consequences to put into my grid) and avoid getting sucked back into trying to decide which side is right.

> Have you written down the mantra from page 35 lately?

The Credibility Spectrum

As you wade back into the shouting match, you probably want to put more weight on statements from credible sources. But because life is full of gray areas, I suggest making a credibility spectrum rather than a simple credible/not credible chart. You can do that by first looking at *who's* saying something (the source) rather than *what's* being said (the statement). Are the sources credible? Do they know what they're talking about? How biased are they likely to be?

> Sources might be an individual, an organization, a newspaper article, a petition, or something else.

For instance, say I'm new in town and am researching which mechanic I want to trust my car to. Before I go asking around, I might establish a credibility spectrum like this:

MORE CREDIBLE

Favorable statements from
competing mechanics

Accounts from trusted friends
who know about cars

Firsthand accounts

Secondhand accounts

LESS CREDIBLE

A naked credibility spectrum for choosing a mechanic.

I call this a naked credibility spectrum because its structure is established for comparing the credibility of different sources but it doesn't yet have any sources placed on it. As I go about looking for advice, I can then place the various statements I hear on that spectrum, based on *who's* saying them rather than *what* is said. This is how you outwit your onboard con man of confirmation bias.

> Sort of like hanging ornaments on the bare branches as you "dress" the Christmas tree.

If I've narrowed the decision down to two candidates, I can place all the statements I've found on one or the other side of the spectrum (I call this dressing the credibility spectrum) and then take a look at the big picture, as on the next page.

For example, the single recommendation for mechanic B from a competing mechanic more than cancels out the three secondhand recommendations for mechanic A. There are, of course, no guarantees. But I can go with mechanic B and feel

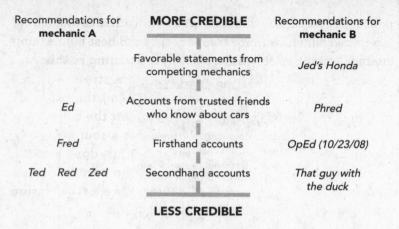

<table>
<tr><td>Recommendations for
mechanic A</td><td>**MORE CREDIBLE**</td><td>Recommendations for
mechanic B</td></tr>
</table>

Recommendations for **mechanic A**	**MORE CREDIBLE**	Recommendations for **mechanic B**
	Favorable statements from competing mechanics	*Jed's Honda*
Ed	Accounts from trusted friends who know about cars	*Phred*
Fred	Firsthand accounts	*OpEd (10/23/08)*
Ted Red Zed	Secondhand accounts	*That guy with the duck*
	LESS CREDIBLE	

A dressed credibility spectrum for choosing a mechanic.

confident that I've made the best bet I can with the time I've been able to give to making the decision.

This process of hanging statements onto a naked credibility spectrum is tremendously powerful because it allows multiple statements to build up an overall picture, which is much more reliable than one or two stunning statements on either side. This helps avoid the inclination to allow a seeming knockout blow—like "Sea levels have actually been dropping over the last two years" (global warming is false!) or "This summer showed record melting of the polar ice cap" (global warming is going to eat your lunch!)—to have veto power over the bigger picture. It's sort of like sighting in a rifle—a single shot doesn't tell you much about what your sights are doing, but several shots can give you a pretty decent indication of what's going on.

Recall red flag 9 on page 70.

This is a way to extract from the shouting match the probabilities and consequences you'll put into your decision grid. Voilà! Your grid then dodges the problem of the giant mutant space hamsters, and you don't feel like you got lost in a sea of conflicting recommendations to make it hap-

Page 30.

pen. Then you can (you hope) come up with a confident answer as to which column in your grid is the best bet, without ever having to decide who's right in the shouting match.

The credibility spectrum also reduces the stress of feeling like you need to get it right when evaluating the reliability of a single source. Because you are going for the big picture, you don't have to fret about exactly where a source goes on the spectrum ("Half an inch higher? Oh, I just don't know!"), since any errors will get washed out by the overall balance. Close enough is close enough, and that takes a lot of pressure off, so you won't hesitate to use the spectrum.

Credibility Factors

Because, as far as I know, I totally made up the idea of the credibility spectrum, there is no correct version. At the end of this chapter, I provide space for you to construct your *own* credibility spectrum to use in the global warming debate.

> Who the heck am I to say what's what?

This is the first step in the "drawing your own conclusions" process that I promised at the outset and that will develop over the remainder of the book.

To combat confirmation bias, I suggest that before you create your naked credibility spectrum, you first think through what factors have an effect on a source's credibility for you. This will help you decide which types of sources to place high or low. And then later, when you go looking for statements to put on your naked credibility spectrum, you can use those factors to figure out where in the chart to place each statement's source.

The factors I use are of course based on my own experiences and values. The factors you use will be based on your own. I offer you my factors—and the credibility spectrum that results—not because I'm right but to illustrate the process. You will come up with your own factors when you make your credibility spectrum.

EXPERTISE

The first factor I use for establishing credibility is expertise.

How much do the sources know about what they are doing? Are they trained? Are they speaking about their own field of study? Are they conscientious? Are they new or long established? Well known or obscure? Is it a meteorologist or a climatologist speaking about climate? Is it an economist speaking about science or a scientist speaking about economics? In other words, how likely are they to arrive at a correct conclusion?

> Meteorologists study short-term and local-scale weather. Climatologists study long-term and large-scale weather patterns, so the latter tend to have more expertise on the subject of climate change.

BIAS

The second factor is the potential for bias. How likely are the sources to put spin on their conclusions? Might they have an agenda of some sort? What do they have to gain or lose by me believing them? For instance, I don't put much weight on someone's recommendation of a product if that person makes a living selling it. I give more weight to a third party's recommendation and even more weight if a *competitor* contradicts his own normal bias and says, "You know, don't tell my boss I said this, but the other guy's product really does the job better."

TRACK RECORD

What is this source's track record? If you can dig it up, how reliable have its recommendations and evaluations proved in the past? Has the source come around to agree with a view it used to oppose? (That's not always a damning thing. In fact, it can be a sign of rationality. But it may be a guide for how much to bet on that source's advice now.) What has been the trend in its assessments?

Some track records are easier to dig up than others. Because petitions aren't really institutions, you'd have to sleuth out the track record of each signer. But for professional organizations or think tanks, it's probably pretty easy to go to their websites (or Wikipedia) and take a look at what they've said in the past and how their recommendations panned out.

I've found that the skeptic and warmer blogs do an excellent job of documenting the track records of the individuals on the other side. I list some of the most prominent blogs at the end of the book, and I highly recommend you use them to look up the track record of any individual or organization whose statements you are evaluating.

Do you remember the Iraqi minister of information during the U.S. invasion of Baghdad in April 2003? Even as reporters could hear the U.S. tanks rumbling outside, the minister held to the official line, proclaiming that any report of U.S. troops in the city was a hoax! Not so credible.

There's no one more reliable in pointing out your mistakes than your opponent!

AUTHORITY

The authority factor raised some hackles when I used it in my videos. A number of critics dismissed my suggestion of examining what experts say by calling that suggestion an "argument from authority," which is a classic logical fallacy. And it's true that in formal logic systems with axioms and well-codified rules—such as mathematics—appealing to an authority is not a valid way to demonstrate the correctness of an idea. But science, with its uncertainty and its dealings with the messy physical world, is not a formal logic system.

As we saw in Chapter 2, authority counts in science. That doesn't mean any given statement from an authority is correct. But such a statement is more likely to be true than one from a lesser authority. Galileo was right in the end when he contradicted the scientific authority of the time (Aristotle's writings interpreted by the church). But history has shown that Galileos are few and far between.

For individual scientists, you can get a sense of their authority by looking up how often other scientists cite their work, meaning how often articles written by other scientists refer to the published papers of the scientist in question. It's a lot like the votes for prom queen or king in high school, except it's more nerd queen or king because it's based on respect for the quality of the scientist's work instead of social popularity.

Publish or Perish is a free program that will do the footwork for you by surveying Google Scholar and giving you the H-Index for an individual scientist (roughly interpreted as how often others cite this scientist's typical paper). This is a single number that the scientific community itself uses as a measure of a scientist's accomplishments, and it turns out to be closely related to a scientist's being awarded a Nobel Prize or being elected to the U.S. National Academy of Sciences, the two biggest honors one can receive in science.

Available at www.harzing .com/pop.htm.

You can get a sense of the authority of peer-reviewed journals by looking up their Article Influence scores at www .eigenfactor.org. This, too, is a single number, which can be roughly interpreted as the number of times scientists cite the average paper in that journal. The Article Influence score is similar to the older Impact Factor—which is what the scientific community generally uses—but is more accessible to us lay people because it doesn't require a subscription to find it. Some journals don't have an Article Influence score (or Impact Factor) because their articles are cited too infrequently to be calculated. This is generally an indication of having extremely little authority in the scientific community.

No one assigns any of these numbers. They are calculated by that final measure of whether a bit of scientific work has merit—does anyone pick it up and run with it? Basically, the higher the number, the greater the authority other scientists give to that individual or journal.

REPUTATION TO PROTECT

What kind of reputation is this source putting on the line by making a particular statement? This is why I trust established mechanics more than brand-new ones; I have greater confidence that they plan on still being in town a couple years from now and don't want to tick off too many people, as opposed to a fly-by-night operation, which has less invested in keeping its name clear. The H-Index or Article Influence score might help give you a sense of how much of a reputation the scientist or journal is putting on the line when making a statement or publishing a paper; a source with a greater reputation to protect might tend to make more conservative (less risky) statements. How long a source has been around can also help you make an assessment; generally, the longer the source's history, the greater reputation it has to protect.

A Beautiful Rainbow of Credibility

Of course, there's a lot of overlap and interplay among these factors, and nothing is for certain. But here's my best shot at a credibility spectrum. (For what it's worth, when I contacted scientists and authors asking for critiques of this, I heard the same criticism from both warmers and skeptics—that my spectrum ends up giving too much credibility to the other side!) The levels on my spectrum are as follows:

Does being disliked by both sides in a polarized debate mean you've found the middle ground? Or that you're just out to lunch? You decide!

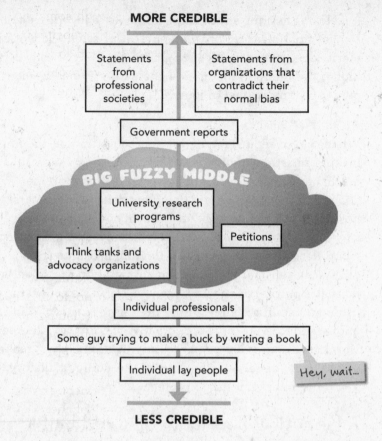

A naked credibility spectrum for the global warming debate.

INDIVIDUAL LAY PEOPLE

At the bottom (least credible), I put individual lay people. We are quite susceptible to bias, and we don't have expertise in climate science or economics, the two main fields in this debate. That's not to say there's nothing to be learned from individuals. They can be useful for insights or for prompting a new way of seeing things, which is why you'll see me quote them. It's just that you don't want to rely on their information any more than is necessary.

I generally put blogs at this level, though sometimes it's hard to tell whether a slick website is mostly the work of one person (and so would go at this level) or the work of an organization, in which case it might go higher up on the spectrum. Do your best.

See Think Tanks and Advocacy Organizations on page 130.

A NOTE ABOUT INDIVIDUALS

Here's a heads up about something you'll hear as you wade out into the shouting match. *Ad hominem* is Latin for "to the man" and is another logical fallacy. It means you try to sway your audience by attacking the source making the statement instead of attacking the statement. "You shouldn't believe this guy because he tortures kittens"—that sort of thing.

Like "argument from authority" on page 81.

Again, in a formal logic system, it's a no-no, and in the climate change debate, you'll find people dismissing each other's arguments by accusing each other of ad hominem attacks. But when establishing credibility, not every statement about an individual is such attack. Saying someone lacks credibility because he's a jerk, and saying someone lacks credibility because she claims the moon is made of cheese are two different things. The first has no bearing on credibility, while the second certainly does (at least in matters of science).

A great example: When it was revealed that Martin Durkin, the maker of the movie *The Great Global Warming Swindle*, had replied in an email to a critic, "Go f*ck yourself," and "You're a daft c*ck," his critics spread those comments widely in an effort to discredit the movie. Hearing that, you should recognize it as an ad hominem attack on Durkin and, therefore, a slimy (and invalid) attempt to reduce the movie's credibility in your mind. However, when Durkin later acknowledged that his team had falsified some data on a key graph used in the movie, then it *was* appropriate to reevaluate the movie's credibility; even though the revelation was about the actions of individuals, it had a bearing on the reliability of the movie's content.

INDIVIDUAL PROFESSIONALS

Above individual lay people I place individual professionals in the field of concern—here climate science or economics. As individuals, they are still susceptible to bias (though less than a lay person, because scientific training explicitly involves training in how to recognize and avoid bias), but at least they have more expertise—provided, that is, that they are speaking about their field or a closely related one. Eliminating bias is not an explicit part of economists' training, so I'm not sure it's fair to say that professionals in this field would generally have less bias than a lay person. But at least they have training in one of the two main fields in the debate—science and economics.

More on economists' training later.

I'm not sure where to put scientists who are speaking about climate science but have no training in or academic research experience in climate science. I wouldn't give them as much credibility in the debate as I would a climate scientist, but they at least have scientific training and so are generally more equipped to judge what's going on than the individual lay person.

As mentioned earlier, you can get a sense of the authority of individual scientists by using *Publish or Perish* to determine their H-Index.

THE BIG FUZZY MIDDLE: THINK TANKS, ADVOCACY ORGANIZATIONS, PETITIONS, AND PROGRAMS

The next few categories I place higher still, but as much as I've thought it through, I haven't been able to rank one above the others, so I'll just lump them all together, floating around the middle somewhere.

Think tanks and advocacy organizations—like the Cato Institute and Greenpeace—are somewhere in the middle. They've definitely got an agenda, but they've also got greater resources than just a single person and so can be more thorough, increasing the expertise factor. On the other hand, because many of them were formed specifically to advance a particular point of view, their bias is probably increased as well. To assess their credibility, consider taking into account how much they want to protect their reputation by not making claims that later end up sounding silly.

Another category I'd put in the Big Fuzzy Middle is petitions and other self-selecting statements, like the 31,000-signature Global Warming Petition Project document and the 1,700-signature U.S. Scientists and Economists' Call for Swift and Deep Cuts in Greenhouse Gas Emissions document. The signers may very well know what they're doing, but the big problem is that they are self-selected; by definition, there are no dissenters on the petition, so the bias factor can be quite significant. Plus they aren't really organizations, so there's no institutional reputation to protect or track record to look up.

One way to give weight to a petition is to look at the signers. Who are they? Are they speaking about their own field? Have they made their names and affiliations public (that is, put their reputation on the line)? What sort of authority do they have (Nobel Prize winner vs. Mr. Someguy)?

I've found that it is essential to do a little looking beyond the simple title of the petition and the number of signers because there are petitions out there of radically different credibilities. Fortunately, you don't need to mount a full-on research project because just the first few minutes of looking into the story behind the petition tends to give you a pretty good idea of the credibility of the statement.

As to the number of signers, for me quality is more important than quantity. All it takes is money and time to get a ton of low-quality signatures, but that doesn't necessarily make the statement more credible.

If the names and affiliations of the signers are disclosed, you can look into their track records, expertise, and authority if you have the time. If the names aren't disclosed, then that might affect how much credibility you assign the petition. It makes a significant difference to me—I find anonymity way less credible than full disclosure.

Probably higher up in the Big Fuzzy Middle I'd place university research programs, like Stanford's Energy Modeling Forum (which looks at the economics involved in climate change policies, among other things) or the Yale Project on Climate Change. I think they are generally more credible than think tanks because they're a couple of funding steps removed from vested interests. They've definitely got expertise and reputations to protect, though they might be founded on the pursuit of some principle, like free markets or environmental stewardship, so bias can still be a bit of a factor. Their track records should be pretty easy to look up, if you're so inclined.

GOVERNMENT REPORTS

The leaders of governments who request major reports are masters of bias, but the bureaucrats and scientists who produce the reports tend not to be. Thus, I rate the bias factor of such reports fairly low. In terms of expertise, God knows the government is big enough to employ quite a number of experts, particularly those who are in professions that have a limited number of available jobs in the private sector, such as scientists and economists.

Large reports typically have so many different people producing them and so many different stakeholders scrutinizing them that the process functions a little bit like the peer-review process. The authors tend to be conservative in reporting their findings (they don't want to overstate the results) and fairly confident. So I generally put government reports fairly high up on the credibility spectrum.

PROFESSIONAL SOCIETIES AND SOURCES THAT CONTRADICT THEIR NORMAL BIAS

At the very top of the credibility spectrum, I put two types of sources that carry the most weight, and I don't think I'd rank one over the other. One category is a statement from an organization that contradicts its normal bias. For instance, if the local timber lobby said, "We've got to thin out this forest for its own health," I wouldn't be that convinced that it would make the forest healthy. But if the Sierra Club made the same statement, I'd sit up and take notice—the reasons must be really compelling if the Sierra Club is going to contradict its normal message.

Finally, sharing that top spot are statements from professional societies—organizations that exist not to advance a particular agenda but to simply serve the communication and training needs of a particular profession, like the American Medical Association in medicine and the American Institute of Architects in building stuff. With these groups, bias and political leanings are going to be as small as can be expected in any human endeavor.

The level of expertise is fairly high because these groups are made up of people who know more about the field than anyone else; furthermore, for such an association to come out with a statement, most of the members would need to agree with it, so what you're getting is general agreement from a whole bunch of experts—no small thing. And the longer an organization has been around or the more prestigious it is, the bigger the reputation it has to protect. You can be fairly confident that an organization has been quite thorough in making sure it doesn't say something that later makes it look silly.

For instance, in 2006, the American Association of Petroleum Geologists (AAPG) changed its official statement on global warming (which rejected the idea of human influence on climate) in response to complaints from a significant number of its members who disagreed with it. The controversy was sparked by the association's presentation of its Journalism Award to Michael Crichton for his novel *State of Fear* (which portrayed global warming as a hoax created by professional scientists in the interest of job security) and involved AAPG members not renewing their memberships because of the statement. As a result, the association adopted a new, more neutral statement on climate change.

So when you see a statement from a professional society, it doesn't mean that every single member agrees with it. But if the statement is far enough out of whack from what the general membership believes, the organization will eventually put it back into whack.

In short, professional societies make up the greatest collection of experts on the planet, with massive reputations on the line, easy-to-check track records, and the least amount of bias you can expect from a group made of fallible humans. That's why in my opinion professional societies are the most credible sources—because when it comes to finding out what science knows, I can't come up with anything that would rank higher. Lord knows these groups aren't perfect. But they are simply as good as it gets.

A DISSENTING VOICE

Not everyone agrees with the weight I give to the statements issued from professional societies, most Page 137. notably the prominent skeptic Richard Lindzen, who is a climatologist at MIT and has written a number of pieces on the matter in the *Wall Street Journal*. Early on in the process of writing this book, I contacted him, asking if he thought my credibility spectrum was a valid way for the lay person to sort through all the contradictory statements around this issue. We had an extensive discussion, particularly about my placing scientific societies at the top of my spectrum.

A few months later, he posted a paper online in which he examines "conscious efforts to politicize science via [the] influence of such bodies," arguing that scientific societies (most notably the National Academy of Sciences) have been infiltrated by "environmental activists" and "global warming alarmists," which makes their statements suspect.

Page 108.

A Word (or Two) About Economics

The basic objection to, Why not take action to fight dangerous climate change, just in case it's true? is generally some version of, Because it would hurt the economy. So economists have become major players in the popular debate in recent years and thus deserve some discussion.

I've heard some people say that listening to economists' opinions on climate change is very much like listening to an HMO accountant's recommendation for which medication to take rather than a doctor's. But I'm not sure that's entirely fair. Economists' expertise about a very critical piece of the big picture should count for something. (After all, what ultimately concerns us about global warming is its impact on our standard of living, which economists study.)

At the same time it's important to remember some key differences between economists and scientists, especially because we are talking about a fundamentally scientific issue. Scientists are specifically trained in how to guard against their own assumptions, but economists are not. So, in general, the profession of economist can be more susceptible to bias than the profession of scientist.

And while all scientists share the assumption that empirical evidence is the final authority, economists must choose to subscribe to one of a variety of schools of thought (Austrian, Keynsian, neoclassical, and so on), each of which is based on unique assumptions, leading to its own conclusions. For instance, one of the choices an economist has to make is how much to "discount" the welfare of people in the future compared to the present, as in, Should the death of a child 20 years from now be weighed the same as the death of a child today? How about 1 year from now? How about in 100 years? This choice of the *discount rate* is fundamentally an ethical decision and can get unpalatable, which is why you rarely hear of it. But almost every economic forecast relies heavily on this choice.

This doesn't mean that economic projections are useless— just that it's worth not taking economic pronouncements with too much confidence, because they are largely determined by assumptions and ethical choices buried in the techno-jargon. Take them as just another bit of information on which to base your risk assessment, not as a reality.

On my credibility spectrum, I generally place economists just below the individual professional level when it comes to the economics of climate change, because they don't have the same training in interpreting the uncertainty in the science of climate change that the scientists do, but they do have expertise relevant to the debate.

Dude, Where's My Science?

Perhaps it has struck you as odd that peer-reviewed articles don't appear anywhere on my credibility spectrum. Here's something surprising: I know I'm writing a book about figuring out a scientific issue and all, but I'm going to encourage you to *not* look into the science. That's because if you don't have scientific training, tracing the arguments through the forest of peer-reviewed literature trying to figure out The Truth is just too ripe for cherry picking by your onboard con man.

For the lay person, it's pretty much like licking a doorknob—chock-full of germs for your confirmation bias. Because there are so many papers available and it is so easy to misinterpret the results, you're bound to find something that confirms your views. And then you're likely to stop, feeling satisfied, because that's how confirmation bias works. In each of us.

Remember Murphy's Law of Research?

You (and I) simply don't have the training to be sufficiently on our guard against misinterpreting things. Recall the discussion and examples in Chapter 2, where I argued how easily the untrained common sense is fooled. That's why it takes a ton of time and coffee to get the letters P, h, and D after your name. Things in science are never as simple as they seem.

Dipping into peer-reviewed articles even briefly makes it too bloody easy to get distracted from your *real* task—deciding what's the best bet and pointing your policy makers in that direction. It's worse than a distraction; it's like touching the tar baby: You just get sucked bit by bit back into the quest to figure out what's true rather than what's the best bet.

Repeat after me, "I don't need to determine who's right."

Scientists use peer-reviewed literature because they've got the training to interpret it, and their job is indeed to pursue what's true. But as a lay person, who am I to say whether principal component analysis is a valid statistical tool for a data series normalized over a subset of the data used as a calibration period chosen based on the reliability of its instrumentation record? I don't even know what that means!

Or, as you recall from Chapter 2, what is as close as we can get to what's true.

As lay people, we don't have the training or the time to dig through the peer-reviewed literature and come up with the big picture. To produce the Intergovernmental Panel on Climate Change (IPCC) report, thousands of experts spent 6 years reviewing the scientific literature to draw some conclusions! I don't know about you, but I don't have that kind of time to figure out what the literature, on balance, says. So it would seem ridiculous for me to read a few peer-reviewed articles and then claim I could make a confident judgment on the overall issue of global warming.

This is the most authoritative report on global warming; for more, see Chapter 6.

I do, however, think it is appropriate to look into the scientific reasoning around the issue if you want to understand a little more about *why* one side makes the claims that it does. Your research won't tell you who's right, but it can help you make a little sense out of what they are saying.

In fact, I've got a whole chapter devoted to that—Chapter 8.

Remember, your job is not to decide which side is right but which column in the grid is a better bet.

So I suggest you resist the temptation to chase the technical arguments back and forth in the literature. Write your mantra, keep your eye on the prize, and avoid getting sucked back into trying to decide which side is right.

Page 35.

Your goal: estimating probabilities and consequences for your grid so that you can make a prudent bet.

Our job here is to be the executives; we are concerned with what direction seems like the best bet in an uncertain setting, even though we are unable to know what's definitely true. As you wade into the shouting match, if you find yourself tempted to evaluate a scientific argument, remember: As a lay person, you don't even need to go there to do your job.

You are the CEO in this picture. Policy makers make up your middle management team, and they are supposed to figure out how to execute the goals you set out for them. And the

I don't want to be the Pointy-Haired Boss.

scientists are your technical employees, who have the training and time to do the research. The peer-reviewed literature is the trade magazine of your business—absolutely necessary to the success of the enterprise but worse than useless in the hands of the executives. In fact, it's downright dangerous. It is simply not in our interest to micromanage.

Sez Who?

In all this careful construction of a credibility spectrum, there's one very important thing to keep in mind: I totally made it up. Yup—just pulled it out of my hat. I've been waving it around for a while, and so far it has stood up pretty well. But hey—I'm just some guy, near the bottom of the spectrum.

So now it's time for you to make your own credibility spectrum. I've provided a blank template for you on page 99. And here's one really cool thing about making your own version: There's no way for anyone to argue that his or her chart is more valid than yours! Because—and here's the critical part:

The point of using a credibility spectrum is *not* to argue that your conclusions are more valid than someone else's. The point is to help you defend yourself against that most pernicious and counterproductive snare your brain sets for you: confirmation bias.

The ultimate goal of using a credibility spectrum is not to win an argument but to make a pragmatic decision that serves *you* well.

Making a credibility spectrum helps guard against confirmation bias by establishing *beforehand*—independent of whether you agree with a given statement or not—how much weight to give statements. It is critically important that you devise yours *before* you go looking for evidence.

So, before you turn to the next chapters—which present statements on climate change from various sources—come up with your own naked credibility spectrum. It's the only way to be fair to yourself, and it will help you get your opinions even closer to physical reality than they already are.

Once you have your naked credibility spectrum in hand—and this is equally critical—use it consistently with every statement you find, *regardless of whether the statement disturbs you or pleases you*. Don't let your brain weasel you out of that. That is where the credibility spectrum's power comes in: helping us get around an inescapable (but manageable) part of our human psyche. That is why it is useful to you and helps you make choices that are in your best interest.

And how convenient that we don't all need to agree on the same credibility spectrum. It's customizable. And free!

What a deal!

CREDIBILITY FACTORS

The first step is perhaps the most important: thinking through the question "How will I decide how much credibility I will give to a particular source?" By determining this beforehand, you guard against having your confirmation bias creep in when you come across a source that says something you like, because you will already have some guidelines. Use the template on page 97 to go through a similar process as I did on pages 79–83, but this time it will be based on your own values

FACTORS THAT INFLUENCE
THE CREDIBILITY OF A SOURCE

Factor:

Details:*

Factor:

Details:

Factor:

Details:

Factor:

Details:

Factor:

Details:

*Reasons the factor influences credibility, examples of how it would
increase or decrease credibility, and so on.*

and experiences, so that everything that flows from this will be custom-fit for you.

TYPES OF SOURCES

On a separate sheet of paper, brainstorm types of sources that you might expect to encounter as you hear about (or research) climate change. Limit this to *types* of sources (media commentators) rather than *actual* sources (Bill O'Reilly, Keith Olbermann), which you will put on in Chapter 10. I listed eight types of sources on my credibility spectrum. Your spectrum might include religious or spiritual leaders, political leaders, media commentators, and newspaper editorialists. The order in which you list them isn't important at this point.

YOUR NAKED CREDIBILITY SPECTRUM

Now for the tough part: ranking the types of sources against each other, based on the factors you identified as influencing credibility. I suggest putting each type of source on its own slip of paper so that you can easily shuffle the sources around before committing to a final order and writing it in this book. On each piece of paper you might want to add some of the details about their credibility factors.

Feel free to have ties or "hazy areas" (like my Big Fuzzy Middle) if it reduces your stress. Remember—details don't count very much here because the eventual purpose is to develop the big picture.

Once you've got your sources in order of credibility, write them on the naked spectrum at right, and include a few bullet points as to why you placed each type of source at its spot on the spectrum. If you have trouble expressing the reasons in terms of your factors, it may be a flag that you should reconsider the location of that source.

MORE CREDIBLE

TYPE OF SOURCE	REASONS FOR PLACING IT AT THIS SPOT

Don't forget to use your credibility factors.

LESS CREDIBLE

CHAPTER 5

GEAR UP:
MUSTERING FOR THE EXPEDITION

Stop! Did you create your naked credibility spectrum in the last chapter? Do that before wading back into the shouting match. It is one of the most useful tools for coming to a decision about global warming that will best serve your interests.

You probably came to this book as a refugee from the shouting match, fed up with the din of overconfident and contradictory warnings and looking to make sense of the senseless: Don't panic—it's a hoax! Panic—it's the greatest threat humanity has ever faced!

So now that you've gotten a rest from the shouting match for half a book, I'm going to throw you back in. But this time, you're ready. You're not going to let all those eggheads and enviro-Nazis and neocon thugs and corporate shills intimidate you, because you've done some *serious training*. You're focused! You know exactly what you're looking for! And you've got solid defensive skills! You're a *Climate Commando*!　Hoo-ah!

THE CLIMATE COMMANDO . . .	COMMANDO SKILLS
. . . is focused!	You know that the most effective question about global warming is not, Is it true? but, Given the risks and uncertainties, what is the most prudent thing to do?
. . . knows exactly what he's looking for!	As you wade into the shouting match, you are hunting quarry for your grid: an estimate of the likelihood of the rows and the contents of the boxes.
. . . has solid defensive skills!	You have an understanding of the nature of science, an awareness of your own confirmation bias, and a credibility spectrum for putting the contrary statements in perspective.

Doing a Sample Problem on the Board

You are about to enter here:

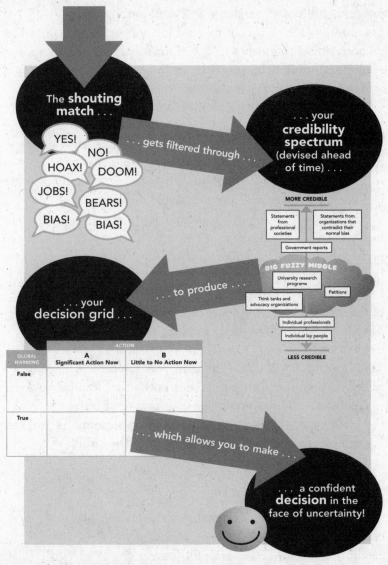

The process of turning uncertainty into confidence.

In the next two chapters, I provide you with statements from the main players in the global warming debate. Of course, there are enough statements out there to fill a whole book. So I went looking for sources as high up on my credibility spectrum as possible, on both sides. There aren't a ton of those, so I am also including statements that—while further down on my spectrum—play a large role in the popular shouting match.

Or, in fact, a World Wide Web.

Chapter 6 contains statements from warmers, and Chapter 7 contains statements from skeptics. In Chapter 8, I explore the reasoning behind the warmers' claims and try to make some sense of why they're all worked up about a degree or two, because this just seems unreasonable to the casual observer.

Hey, sometimes I feel kinda chilly.

My selections are by no means complete, because all I'm really doing is giving you an example of how to go about applying the tools of risk management that I've suggested in this book. Essentially, I'm doing a sample problem on the board. If I instead tried to present an evenhanded and final assessment of the issue, then I would just be one more voice shouting, "Believe *me*!" And you're likely reading this book because you're tired of that.

So, while I *will* share my own conclusion in Chapter 9, I offer you an opportunity to work out the problem for yourself in Chapter 10. There, you'll use your *own* credibility spectrum, the sources I've presented, and any other statements you feel are important but that I didn't include in the book.

Adapt vs. Mitigate

My lumping of a complex debate into just two camps—warmer and skeptic—is, of course, incredibly reckless. Here's a slightly more detailed view of the various skeptical beliefs:

Whenever you try to simplify a complex topic, there's bound to be some uncomfortable squishing.

1. The globe isn't warming.

2. The globe is warming, but humans aren't causing it.

3. We're warming the globe, but the change is not significant.

4. The globe is warming, but it's too big to fix. We'd be better off working to adapt to the changes rather than trying to prevent them.

The warmers say the globe is warming, we're the ones doing it, it's significant, and we can still do something to reduce the severity. While there have been warmers trumpeting that view since the very start of the debate 30 years ago, the skeptics have tended to progress through all the listed points in sequence. (It makes sense, really, because why risk the economy unless you're confident that global warming is real *and* caused by us *and* a bad thing *and* significant *and* fixable?)

Most skeptics these days have progressed to number 4, saying, "Adapt" (focus efforts on protecting ourselves from the changes in climate, like building dikes around coastal cities to hold back rising sea levels), while the warmers are saying, "Mitigate" (focus efforts on trying to make the changes smaller, like keeping the sea level from rising in the first place by cutting carbon emissions).

In practice, both camps generally call for some level of adaptation *and* mitigation. Most of the warmers are convinced that we're already in for some significant climate change, so we're going to have to do some adapting even if we cut emissions radically to prevent worse changes. And some skeptics (though not all) say that emission cuts aren't a bad thing in themselves—it's just mandatory cuts that are harmful to the economy and should be avoided. So the difference is on emphasis.

The Tool Kit: Checklist of Equipment

We are about to wade into what can be an emotional minefield because it is chock-full of stuff that plays directly to the base of our brain: fear and uncertainty. Over the last three chapters, you've acquired some substantial equipment to guard against having your brain's pitfalls influence your choice of lottery tickets in the global warming gamble. So before we enter the drop zone, let's check our gear. Make sure you've got everything on this list:

- [ ] A laser-like **focus on your ultimate goal**—building a *decision grid* to help you figure out what is the best bet in this wager.

- [ ] A *mantra* to help you **avoid** getting sucked back into the desire to figure out **who's right in the debate** and a *red pen* to write that mantra at the top of every page (page 35).

- [ ] An *understanding* of the **uncertain nature of science** and that nothing can ever be proven; whether an issue has been demonstrated sufficiently depends on the stakes involved (page 38).

- [ ] An *understanding* of **authority in science**, both the role it plays and how it is determined (page 46).

- [ ] *Red flags* installed in your brain to help you **guard against** your onboard con man, **confirmation bias** (page 68).

- [ ] *Strategies* for **countering** possible **confirmation bias** if one of those flags goes up (page 71).

- [ ] A *credibility spectrum* of your own devising, made without regard to any particular statements on climate change and based on your own **criteria established**

ahead of time and applied equally to *all* statements (pages 99 and 97, respectively).

☐ A *tolerance* for **some uncertainty**, without stressing out too much about exactly where to place a source on the credibility spectrum, **because what counts** in the end is **the big picture**.

You're not going to do this in one sitting, so whenever you pick up this book to read something in Chapters 6 and 7 (or whenever you come across new stuff from any source), briefly review this list to keep yourself on track.

The Selection of Sources

The selection of statements in the next two chapters is not comprehensive but is a starting point. I tried to find sources to fill in my credibility spectrum from the top down. On each side there is a wealth—okay, an oversupply—of sources that belong at the bottom of the spectrum. But because I don't give those much credibility, I didn't want to bother grabbing a bunch of that stuff if I could find more credible sources located higher up on the spectrum.

I have included the most credible sources I could find on both sides of the spectrum. In addition, I've included some sources that are low on my spectrum but quite visible in the popular debate, so that when you happen to come across them out there in the shouting match, you can see where they fit in *my* picture.

If you think I left off an important source due to my own bias and cherry picking, I can assure you that any flagrant omissions are the result of simple incompetence and lack of sleep. But I guess that's a lot like the whole global warming issue: We may not be able to afford to wait until we've completed our research before we need to give an answer. So we go with what we've got. As economist Herman Daly put it, "If you jump out of an airplane you need a crude parachute more than an accurate altimeter."

Consider this sort of a program of players in a game—a great starting place to get the lay of the land and get ideas for areas to look into further. The next chapters should not, however, be taken as *the* authoritative compilation of sources of information.

A Friendly Warning

For each source, I tell you where I would place it on my own credibility spectrum and why. But because I—like any human—am bound to be biased despite my best efforts to be evenhanded, I want to explicitly warn you: Don't take my descriptions of the sources as truth but only as a starting place. I am sharing with you why *I* place the sources where I do on *my* credibility spectrum. This is a sample problem, after all, not The Truth. You will have a chance to do your own assessment of the sources on your own credibility spectrum in Chapter 10.

Your being aware of my fallibility is particularly important if there has been any controversy associated with a source or its statements. The mere existence of a controversy doesn't affect the source's credibility in my mind, but the content of the controversy might have some influence on the source's credibility (if there is fraud, conflict of interest, or severe bias). Some of those controversies have had an effect on where I placed the source on my credibility spectrum, but I think you should make your own judgment.

> All it takes is a baseless smear campaign on the other side to create a "controversy."

I will note when there is a significant amount of controversy around a source's statements, so you can go do your own research. Wikipedia is a great place to start, though you

And is an index of further places to investigate.

shouldn't take it as truth—it offers only an overview. Just remember to be *especially* on your guard about your own confirmation bias as you investigate your sources. Researching controversies is like a candy store for your onboard con man, because as you chase the arguments back and forth, it is just so bloody *easy* to simply stop when you hear something that confirms your opinion instead of continuing on to look for the rebuttal to that point.

Remember: When I point out that there has been controversy, that in itself doesn't affect the source's credibility. Einstein was controversial. So were Stalin and Newton and Gandhi and the Reverend Jim Jones and Donald Duck (the no-pants thing). I'm simply giving you a heads-up that you may want to look into the source a bit more closely.

A WHOLE COOP OF CHICKEN LITTLES: STATEMENTS FROM WARMERS

You're better off reading firsthand what someone said than reading what I said he or she said. So when I put together this survey of warmers' statements, my inclination was to minimize my commentary and mostly provide just quotes from those sources. But when I did that, I ended up with an impenetrable wad of disjointed quotations.

> Even my dedicated wife said that it made her eyes glaze over.

So instead, I decided to focus on identifying the sources and explaining their location on my credibility spectrum. A couple of chapters ago I talked about credibility factors, such as expertise, likelihood of bias, track record, authority, and reputation to protect. In this chapter, I summarize my sources' statements as objectively as I can, but I encourage you to go to www.gregcraven.org to read some long excerpts I've pulled from the original statements. This way you can backstop my potentially biased characterizations without having to spend hours and hours combing the Internet or reading 200-page reports.

> The version of this chapter that made my wife's eyes glaze over.

Got your gear from the last chapter? Here, finally, you wade back into the shouting match. Take a deep breath and keep your eye on the prize: likelihoods and consequences for your decision grid.

> Written your mantra lately?

Professional Societies

NATIONAL ACADEMY OF SCIENCES (NAS)

Remember how authority is earned in science? Election to the U.S. National Academy of Sciences (NAS)

> Page 46.

is the greatest statement of respect that can be given to a scientist by his or her peers. It was founded by Abraham Lincoln in 1863, and 1 in 10 of its members is a Nobel Prize winner. Through its research arm—the National Research Council (NRC)—the academy summarizes the body of peer-reviewed literature in reports such as *Abrupt Climate Change*, mentioned later in the chapter.

I am not saying that the NAS is perfect. But it seems to me that if I'm ever going to believe anything science has to say, it would be what these guys tell me. Members of the NAS provide, quite literally, the best that science has to offer.

It is made of humans, after all.

In 2005, the NAS and the science academies of the other industrialized nations jointly issued an official statement claiming that "the threat of climate change is clear and increasing." They called on nations to take action now, claiming that waiting any longer would only make our inevitable response more expensive, with greater negative consequences because of accelerating climate change.

The NAS goes at the top of my credibility spectrum because of its unique position in the scientific community, its long history, its membership (the best scientists from all fields), its track record, and the unrivaled reputation it has to protect.

AMERICAN ASSOCIATION
FOR THE ADVANCEMENT OF SCIENCE (AAAS)

The American Association for the Advancement of Science (AAAS; known as "triple-A, S") is the largest scientific society in the world, with 144,000 members. It's been around since before the U.S. Civil War and is the publisher of the journal *Science*—the gold standard for peer-reviewed journals. What the American Medical Association (AMA) is to the field of medicine, AAAS is to the field of science. In terms of authority in science, it is second only to the NAS.

In 2006, AAAS issued an official position statement that called climate change a clear and growing threat to society. The association claimed that the pace of climate change has increased in recent years and said that "the intensification of droughts, heat waves, floods, wildfires, and severe storms" are "early warning signs of even more devastating damage to come, some of which will be irreversible."

Like the NAS, AAAS noted that taking action now to control emissions is cheap compared to the costs of delaying: "The longer we wait to tackle climate change, the harder and more expensive the task will be . . . with a mounting toll on vulnerable ecosystems and societies."

I put AAAS at the top of my credibility spectrum because of its unique role in the scientific community (the AMA of science), its long history, the weighty reputation it has to protect, and the staggering number of people it is accountable to (who would be expected to rebel if AAAS went too far in its official statements).

Remember the AAPG (page 90)?

NATIONAL RESEARCH COUNCIL (NRC)

In 2002, the National Research Council, the research arm of the NAS, published *Abrupt Climate Change*, which carries the catchy subtitle *Inevitable Surprises*. The book is available in PDF form and can be read online in its entirety.

The book details something that is well-accepted in the scientific community (or at least the authors say so) but little known by the rest of us: that the climate in the past has undergone changes far more rapid and extreme than we had previously imagined—in periods as short as a decade. Such changes were triggered by natural events in the past, and the book warns that we might unintentionally trigger such a rapid change again with our carbon emissions.

"Abrupt climate changes of the magnitude seen in the past

would have far-reaching implications for human society and ecosystems," says the NRC, "including major impacts on energy consumption and water supply demands. Could such a change happen again? Are human activities exacerbating the likelihood of abrupt climate change? What are the potential societal consequences of such a change?"

The book pretty much answers these last three questions with yes, probably, and huge (my words), and it calls for pursuing "no-regrets" strategies (their words).

Statements that come out of the NRC represent the best of what's been distilled from scientific understanding at the time. So this book goes at the top of my credibility spectrum.

Sources That Contradict Their Normal Bias

NATIONAL INTELLIGENCE ASSESSMENT (NIA)

In 2008, all 16 U.S. intelligence agencies, including the CIA, FBI, and National Security Agency (NSA), jointly produced a report known as the National Intelligence Assessment. According to the chairman of the National Intelligence Council (the report itself is classified), the report warns that the economic and environmental pressures of climate change are likely to push already fragile nations over the edge, leading to more wars, which in turn will create millions of refugees and frequent humanitarian crises. The U.S. military would be strained as it was increasingly drawn in to such conflicts, reducing our national security "readiness posture."

> Gotta love the spook-speak.

The assessment points out that these events would disrupt America's access to critical raw materials obtained through international markets, which would also have serious consequences for national security. The report warns of costly threats on the home front as well, including wildfires, storm surges, water shortages, and thawing permafrost in Alaska (which damages the infrastructure).

Any report from this group of agencies would seem to me to be the most competent assessment of threats to the nation that exists. I mean, that's their job. This expertise, combined with the contradicts-normal-bias factor (since the spooks aren't generally known for being green), is why I would promote this assessment from the usual government report to a spot at the top of my spectrum.

THE PENTAGON

In 2003 the Pentagon released a study titled "An Abrupt Climate Change Scenario and Its Implications for United States National Security: Imagining the Unthinkable." It sketches out the national security implications for a worst-case but plausible scenario resulting from abrupt climate change.

The report explores how such an event would destabilize the geopolitical environment, leading to frequent wars over scarce resources. "Disruption and conflict will be endemic features of life," it chirps breezily, observing that "Every time there is a choice between starving and raiding, humans raid." If such an abrupt change in climate occurred, "Humanity would revert to its norm of constant battles for diminishing resources. . . . Once again warfare would define human life."

My favorite line is "With inadequate preparation, the result [of abrupt climate change] could be a significant drop in the human carrying capacity of the Earth's environment" because it makes me wonder, Did they just say, *We're all gonna die!* but in government-speak?

Although this report was not as thorough as the NIA report (it involved fewer people), I place this report at the top of my credibility spectrum as a source that contradicts its normal bias.

CENTER FOR NAVAL ANALYSES (CNA)

The Center for Naval Analyses started in World War II and functions as a think tank serving the needs of the U.S. Navy. In 2007, it released a study called "National Security and the Threat of Climate Change," authored by a group of top-ranking retired military guys—the lowest-ranked guy there was a lieutenant general.

It must have really sucked for him when the other guys kept saying, "Hey kid—go get us some coffee."

The study calls the effects of climate change "potentially devastating" and relates that the group's discussions with climate scientists were lively, informative, "and very sobering." This group of crew cuts called global warming a "threat multiplier" because it would lead to more failed nations (breeding grounds for terrorists and extremists), drawing the United States into more wars. Noting that current carbon levels in the atmosphere are the highest in 650,000 years, the study advises that we should act soon because the risks to national security will "almost certainly" get worse the longer we delay.

That description, coming from career war planners, makes me a little twitchy. I dunno why.

Regarding arguments that we shouldn't take action because the threat is uncertain, one of the panel members, a former U.S. Army chief of staff, remarked, "Speaking as a soldier, we never have 100 percent certainty. If you wait until you have 100 percent certainty, something bad is going to happen on the battlefield."

Another participant, former commander of U.S. forces in the Middle East General Tony Zinni, said, "We will pay for this one way or another. We will pay to reduce greenhouse gas emissions today, and we'll have to take an economic hit of some kind. Or, we will pay the price later in military terms. And that will involve human lives. There will be a human toll."

Given the weighty makeup of the group and the fact that the military is not typically known for getting its shorts in a twist about fluffy environmental concerns, I'd say this report belongs at the top of my credibility spectrum (as a source that contradicts its normal bias) rather than at the think-tank level.

> Just like if the Sierra Club called for a forest to be clear-cut.

CENTER FOR STRATEGIC AND INTERNATIONAL STUDIES (CSIS) AND CENTER FOR A NEW AMERICAN SECURITY (CNAS)

Two separate national security think tanks—the Center for Strategic and International Studies (CSIS) and the Center for a New American Security (CNAS)—collaborated on a 2007 study titled "The Age of Consequences: The Foreign Policy and National Security Implications of Global Climate Change." The team that put it together was a multidisciplinary mix of high muckety-mucks, including the head of the NAS, a Nobel laureate economist, a former CIA director, a former chief of staff to the president,

> And a token historian.

and a former national security adviser to the vice president. Oh yeah, and climatologists, too.

They found that the scientific community has been "shocked at how fast some effects of global warming are unfolding" and called the current projections of climate models "too conservative." "The consequences of even relatively low-end global climate change," the report stated, "include the loosening and disruption of societal networks. At higher ranges of the spectrum, chaos awaits." One of the study participants even cited the Mel Gibson disaster movie *Mad Max* during discussions of the "scientifically plausible" worst-case scenario. The other (less-hip) members simply compared it to the aftermath of a nuclear war between superpowers.

"The question is whether a threat of this magnitude will dishearten humankind, or cause it to rally in a tremendous, generational struggle for survival and reconstruction. . . . If that rally does not occur relatively early on, then chances increase that the world will be committed irrevocably to severe and permanent global climate change at profoundly disruptive levels."

The authors claimed that we need to mount an effective response in less than a decade "in order to have any chance" of preventing irreversible disaster. "We are already in the midst of choosing among alternative futures," they warned.

Although this study was produced by think tanks, the nature of these particular think tanks (focused on national security rather than environmental concerns), plus the membership of the panel—high expertise, high authority, and not inclined to be ecowarriors—has me thinking it belongs at the top of my spectrum as a source that contradicts its normal bias.

U.S. CLIMATE ACTION PARTNERSHIP (USCAP)

In 2007, an unusual collection of companies came together as the U.S. Climate Action Partnership (USCAP) and issued a report centered around a call for government-imposed mandatory carbon emissions caps—*on their own industries*. The coalition includes BP America, Shell, ConocoPhillips, Ford Motor, General Electric, General Motors, Chrysler, Deere, Caterpillar, Dow Chemical, DuPont, Johnson & Johnson, PG&E, Alcoa, and Siemens.

The report is titled "A Call for Action" and is filled with money quotes for someone with a confirmation bias for column A. Perhaps the biggest was the simple early statement: "We know enough to act on climate change." "There must be a reasoned and serious debate about the solutions," the authors continued, "but debate cannot substitute for action."

Like me.

The report contradicted the idea that taking action would harm the economy, claiming instead that the resulting new markets, increased U.S. competitiveness, reduced reliance on energy from foreign sources, increased energy security, and improved balance of trade would all grow the economy.

If we're quick about it.

Like the other reports mentioned in this chapter, this one claims that we have already used up all our lead time: "Each year we delay action to control emissions increases the risk of unavoidable consequences that could necessitate even steeper reductions in the future, at potentially greater economic cost and social disruption." The authors don't underestimate the scale of what's necessary, though, calling it "enormous," and that's why they say that massive government action is necessary to "fundamentally change . . . the way we produce and use energy."

They also explicitly address the skeptical objection of, Well, whatever we do in the United States won't matter since China and India are such big carbon emitters by declaring that "U.S. action to implement mandatory measures and incentives for reducing emissions should not be contingent on simultaneous action by other countries."

This is a remarkable report, given the source. And the statements don't just represent the views of a few individuals but represent those of a ton of economics specialists. Given how so many remarkably strong statements so directly contradict the normal bias of the coalition members (mandatory emissions caps!), I put this source at the top of my credibility spectrum.

GLOBAL CEO LETTER

The work of the CEOs of 80 global corporations over 16 months resulted in the 2008 release of the report "CEO Climate Policy Recommendations to G8 Leaders."

The document emphasized a risk-management approach in the face of any remaining uncertainty about climate change and called for "nothing less than a rapid and fundamental strategy to reach a low-carbon world economy." Like the other statements I've presented here, it emphasized the urgency of the issue, saying, "we do not have much time." I found it significant that the authors wrote, "Climate change is a serious social and economic challenge."

The lack of any mention of The Environment in that sentence highlights how these CEOs see the issue as simply a pragmatic one. And they concluded that it is "a reasonable approach" for all leaders of business and government to cause greenhouse gas emissions to fall very strongly by 2050.

The signatories include the CEOs of Shell, BP, Duke Energy, Michelin, Airbus, British Airways, All Nippon Airways, Alcoa, DuPont, Deutsche Bank, Citibank, Advanced Micro Devices (AMD), Credit Suisse, Bayer, Pricewaterhouse-Coopers, Rolls-Royce, Reuters, and Nike.

Businesses are the most fundamentally self-interested thing out there. (In fact, for publicly traded companies, their legal obligation is to maximize value for their shareholders—nothing else.) So, given the expertise represented by these companies and their normal bias for the bottom line (rather than preserving Mother Earth), if they say action on climate change is in their interests, that significantly increases their credibility. That is why I put this report at the top of my spectrum as a source that contradicts its normal bias.

EXXONMOBIL

ExxonMobil is the largest company in the world and has been considered by many to be the poster child of skeptical activism on global warming. There is even a whole website (ExxonSecrets.org) dedicated to "highlighting the more than a decade-long campaign by Exxon-funded front groups—and the scientists they work with—to deny the urgency of the scientific consensus on global warming and delay action to fix the problem."

Its interactive map of connections is totally engrossing! Way more fun than solitaire on the computer.

But starting in 2007, Exxon stopped funding many of those groups, including the Competitive Enterprise Institute, the Marshall Institute, and the Heartland Institute.

Discussed in Chapter 7.

While Exxon hasn't signed on to either USCAP or the global CEO recommendations, CEO Rex Tillerson did echo both when he said in 2007, "The risks to society and ecosystems from climate change could prove to be significant. So, despite the uncertainties, it is prudent to develop and implement sensible strategies that address these risks," adding that government should be the one to do that.

And a January 2007 *Wall Street Journal* article quotes Exxon's vice president for public affairs, Kenneth Cohen, who was speaking about greenhouse gas emissions and their effect on global temperatures, as saying, "society knows enough now—that the risk is serious and action should be taken."

They may not sound totally gung-ho, but given Exxon's unique history in the debate, these statements go at the top of my spectrum, in the contradicts-normal-bias category.

SHELL OIL

Royal Dutch Shell is the eighth-largest company in the world. In a speech in 2006, president John Hofmeister said, "From Shell's point of view, the debate is over. When 98 percent of scientists agree, who is Shell to say, 'Let's debate the science?'"

And in 2007, CEO Jeroen van der Veer wrote an open letter titled "Two Energy Futures," sketching out two possibilities for the world's energy future. In the business-as-usual scenario, he envisions that carbon emissions would not be seriously addressed until we experience climate shocks, which would trigger severe political reactions and lead to energy price spikes and volatility. As an alternative, he suggested we anticipate the inevitable—that easy supply of oil and gas will no longer meet demand by 2015—and begin moving now to a low-carbon economy through cap-and-trade policies. Perhaps most surprising, he said that companies can make suggestions, "but governments are in the driver's seat."

That's not a typo—yes, 2015.

Given the significant contradicts-normal-bias factor and the size of the company, I would put these statements at the top of my credibility spectrum.

AMERICAN ENTERPRISE INSTITUTE (AEI)

In 2008, the American Enterprise Institute for Public Policy Research (AEI) released a paper titled "Resetting the Earth's Thermostat" that made me nearly fall out of my seat when I read it. That's because AEI is a very influential conservative think tank at the center of efforts to promote skeptical views of global warming. But this paper read like an overwrought warmer hissy fit.

It says that with our carbon emissions, we are currently running a massive, unintentional experiment with the global climate and that there is no other public policy issue for which the potential harm is so large. The paper argues that the consequences of trying to adapt to climate change after it happened would be far worse than taking action to prevent it in the first place.

It warns that by the time there are unmistakable signs of climate disaster, it will be too late to do anything about it except radical, untested things like injecting sulfur particles into the atmosphere to reflect sunlight. While this action itself may very well deplete the ozone layer and disrupt the Asian monsoons, the paper says those effects would be better than uncontrolled climate change.

Even though this is from a think tank (Big Fuzzy Middle), the sharp contrast of the paper's statements with AEI's history contributes significant contradicts-normal-bias factor, so this statement goes high up on my credibility spectrum on the warmer's side.

Government Reports

INTERGOVERNMENTAL PANEL ON CLIMATE CHANGE (IPCC)

The Intergovernmental Panel on Climate Change (IPCC) is the central player in the climate change debate. Every 5 years or so, it produces a synthesis of the current state of the science. It has released four reports, in 1990, 1996, 2001, and 2007. The IPCC is dismissed by many on the skeptical side as a hack political body. But a look at the process the IPCC uses to produce its reports would sure seem to argue that those reports represent the most massive and thorough synthesis of the peer-reviewed literature on the planet, involving "2,500+ scientific expert reviewers, 800+ contributing authors and 450+ lead authors from 130+ countries" working more than 6 years to review thousands of peer-reviewed papers.

The 2007 report called global warming "unequivocal" and said it is "highly likely" due to human activity. The authors gave a huge range of projections depending on what we do: a global temperature rise of 3.2°F to 11.5°F by the year 2100 and a sea level rise of 7 to 23 inches (though it says "the upper values of the range are not to be considered upper bounds for sea level rise," owing to the missing feedbacks I discuss in Chapter 8). The report also predicted the same bundle of negative consequences you're accustomed to hearing about by this point: worsening hurricanes, droughts, floods, wildfires, species extinction, migrating disease patterns, environmental refugees, collapsed fisheries, and the like.

It is perhaps significant to note that over the 15-year course of the IPCC's reports, observed changes in the climate have almost always turned out to be larger and faster than it had projected. This affects my track record factor and argues that its current projections are probably more conservative than what is likely to actually happen.'

Along those lines, it's also worth noting that because of the massive size of the project and the number of sponsoring governments who have to sign off on the final report, the IPCC's findings always lag several years behind the current science at any given time. As noted above, this would seem to argue that things will likely be worse than what the IPCC says. A good illustration of that dynamic comes from the 2007 report's projection that the Arctic could be ice free during summers by the end of the century; as I write this in late 2008, the more up-to-date literature anticipates that the Arctic will be free of summer ice within the next two decades.

On the other hand, many people suspect governments of being driven by a desire to gain more control, and playing up a crisis would serve that. So perhaps the IPCC's findings are biased in favor of making more alarming statements than the science actually merits. As you evaluate that for yourself, it's worth knowing that the IPCC's findings have been endorsed by the statements from AAAS, the NAS, the National Intelligence Assessment, the global CEO recommendations, and others.

Several of the experts I asked to review my credibility spectrum took serious exception that I did not place the IPCC at the very top, and I can see their point. But to guard against my confirmation bias, I'll stick to the principles I laid out for my spectrum and confine the IPCC to the government report level. Despite the existence of several dissenters from within the IPCC (including John Christy), I'll put it at the top of its section because of the sheer scope of its process and Page 140.

the many endorsements it has received by other highly credible sources.

STERN REVIEW

The "Stern Review on the Economics of Climate Change" was prepared at the request of the British government by a working group headed by Sir Nicholas Stern, the former chief economist of the World Bank.

Released in 2006, it caused quite a controversy. The main dispute seems to come down to the choice of the discount rate (a single number) that the Stern committee used. As I explained in Chapter 4, my understanding of this number is that there is no right answer or even a generally accepted answer, but that the choice of what value to use is essentially an ethical choice—how much less does the welfare of a kid 20 years from now count compared to a kid today?

The report concluded that taking action might cost up to 1 percent of the GDP while not taking action might cost up to 20 percent of GDP due to the threat of climate change causing "the greatest and widest-ranging market failure ever seen." Just 2

GDP stands for "gross domestic product" and is the most basic measure of a nation's economy.

years later, in 2008, Stern revised the cost estimate upward from 1 percent to 2 percent of the GDP because newer evidence showed that climate change was happening faster than had been thought and, therefore, costing more to combat. Stern's conclusions seem to support the claim of many of the sources cited earlier in this chapter that delay only makes the inevitable more expensive.

I'd put this fairly high in the government report level of my spectrum. The fact that it was used by the authors of both the National Intelligence Assessment and the global CEO letter helps increase its credibility for me, because neither of those two sources seems particularly flaky.

Petitions

UNION OF CONCERNED SCIENTISTS' 2005 PETITION

A total of 25 "senior economists with expertise in the application of economics to environmental policy" signed a 2005 petition titled "United States Needs Incentive-Based Policy to Reduce Carbon Emissions: Statement by Leading Economists." The signatories include three Nobel laureates and one former member of the President's Council of Economic Advisers.

The statement claimed that "there is now no credible scientific doubt" that global warming is real, human caused, and will be disruptive. It calls for a cap on carbon emissions as a sort of "public insurance policy" despite any remaining uncertainties.

The names and affiliations of the signatories are disclosed, which always increases credibility for me. Page 88. Nevertheless, it's still a petition, and so despite the three Nobel laureates, the statement goes in the Big Fuzzy Middle of my credibility spectrum.

> Three Nobel laureates is nothing to sneeze at. Not that you'd try.

REDEFINING PROGRESS'S 1997 PETITION

Signed by more than 2,500 economists, including nine Nobel Prize winners, the "Economists' Statement on Climate Change" is pretty straightforward: "As economists, we believe that global climate change carries with it significant environmental, economic, social, and geopolitical risks, and that preventive steps are justified."

The petition calls for international, market-based actions, such as a tax on carbon emissions, yet claims that with the right policy decisions, this could address climate change without harming living standards.

The document is fairly old (drafted in 1997), but I include it here because in the intervening years, the picture painted by the increasing understanding of climate science has only gotten more severe and more immediate. So I think it's reasonable to assume that if the signers of the petition advocated action back then, they would advocate action today as well.

The names and affiliations of the signers (including the nine Nobel laureates) are disclosed, so I'd put this petition near the top of the Big Fuzzy Middle.

> Hmm . . . how many Nobel laureates would it take to break out of that cloud? That's a question I'll leave for the philosophers.

UNION OF CONCERNED SCIENTISTS' 2008 PETITION

In 2008, "more than 1,700 scientists and economists with expertise relevant to our understanding of the scientific and economic dimensions of climate change, its impacts, and solutions" endorsed "The U.S. Scientists and Economists' Call for Swift and Deep Cuts in Greenhouse Gas Emissions" petition. The list of signatories includes six Nobel Prize winners in science or economics, 30 members of the National Academy of Sciences, 10 members of the National Academy of Engineering, and 10 recipients of a MacArthur fellowship.

> A MacArthur fellowship is sometimes called a "genius grant." It's unique in that you don't apply for it. You just get a phone call one day saying, "Here's half a million dollars for being such a great addition to humanity."

The eggheads and greenshades said that "the strength of the science on climate change compels us to warn the nation about the growing risk of irreversible consequences." They called for swift action that would result in an 80 percent reduction in emissions by 2050, which they assert is "achievable and consistent with sound economic policy." They emphasize that the policies should be mandatory because voluntary initiatives have shown themselves in the past to be ineffective.

Like other statements, this one claims that limiting and adapting to climate change will only get more expensive with every passing year: "There is no time to waste. The most risky thing we can do is nothing."

The signatories and their affiliations are all disclosed, and with so many credentialed heavyweights on the rolls, I put this statement fairly high up in the Big Fuzzy Middle of my spectrum.

Individual Professionals

JAMES HANSEN

James Hansen is the climatologist who kicked off the public debate with his testimony to Congress in 1988, and he has been at the center of the shouting match ever since. He has a track record of saying things publicly about global warming that the skeptics ridicule and even mainstream scientists say, "Well, I don't know if I'd go *that* far." But as the science advances, the mainstream does indeed end up going that far. This keeps happening, which would seem to make Hansen a decent indication for what the well-established scientific understanding might be saying a few years from now.

In fact, I poked around the climate science community a bit, asking if anyone could give me another scientist with a better track record than Hansen, and no one did. So I guess as a bellwether, Hansen must be one of the best we've got.

But don't just believe me. Go ask your own scientists. If you find a better bellwether than Hansen, please tell me at www.gregcraven.org.

His public statements have gotten increasingly strident as the science has progressed, and he is now saying that even the most ambitious targets on the planet for emissions cuts—the 2008 European Union goals, which were themselves based on his earlier work—guarantee us a climate disaster.

An explanation of what those numbers mean is in Chapter 8. For now, it's enough to know that the number 350 implies reductions in carbon emissions that are radically more aggressive than any policy makers are currently talking about.

In a peer-reviewed paper in 2008, Hansen and his team wrote: "If humanity wishes to preserve a planet similar to that on which civilization developed and to which life on Earth is adapted, CO_2 will need to be reduced from its current 385 ppm to at most 350 ppm."

With his unrivaled track record and the authority implied by how often his papers are cited by other scientists, I would place him high in the individual professional level of my spectrum. It is significant to me that his conclusions are primarily based not on computerized climate models—a common target for skeptic's criticisms of doomsday scenarios—but on studies of what the climate has actually done in the distant past. That seems much more resistant to easy criticism.

NAOMI ORESKES

A geologist and science historian, Naomi Oreskes is the author of the 2004 peer-reviewed study that was alluded to in the movie *An Inconvenient Truth,* which surveyed the scientific literature on global warming and found no peer-reviewed papers that contradicted the view that humans are causing the globe to warm significantly. Her findings were challenged by British social scientist Benny Peiser, and controversy ensued. In 2007, Oreskes gave a lecture that made Page 145. the warmer rounds on YouTube. In it she detailed the alleged organized campaign to create doubt and confusion on the issue, using the same people who ran such a campaign for the tobacco companies.

Although she is not a climate scientist, her training in a

hard science (PhD in geology) and her re-search focus on the nature of scientific consensus and dissent would put her at the individual professional level of my spectrum.

Can you say "global warming debate"?

Individual Lay People

AL GORE AND AN INCONVENIENT TRUTH

Of course, we can't leave this chapter without mentioning the Goremeister. Former Vice President Al Gore's movie *An Inconvenient Truth* made a big splash when it came out in 2006, and won the Oscar for best documentary as well as garnering Gore a Nobel Peace Prize (shared with the IPCC) in 2007. There has been so much bitter debate around the film that I don't think it's very useful to use for my analysis.

I am including it here because I think it is important to see how small a part such movies actually play when trying to estimate likelihoods and consequences about the physical world. I'd place Gore just below individual professional because, although he's not a scientist or an economist, he did enough homework to qualify for a promotion from individual lay person.

CHAPTER 7

EVERYTHING'S GOING TO BE JUST FINE: STATEMENTS FROM SKEPTICS

The policy debate often simplifies into one of science and economics. The warmers say, "Climate change may not be certain, but why not take action anyway, just in case it turns out to be really dangerous?" And the skeptics reply, "Because it would be too expensive to be worth guarding against an uncertain threat."

You already know from my disclaimer in Chapter 0 that I'm a warmer. In an effort to neutralize my bias as much as possible, I enlisted the help of climate skeptics in attacking my own argument. I am familiar enough with science to be confident that I could find the major skeptical sources in the scientific community, but I know next to nothing about economics. So that's what I asked the skeptics for help on—finding some very credible sources to help fill in the top left box of my decision grid (we took action on climate change but didn't need to)—because that is a main focus of skeptical arguments for not taking action ("It would be too expensive to be worth it").

Trying to stir up significant effort, I challenged skeptics to find good sources predicting dire economic consequences. I put the challenge in the comments to my "The Most Terrifying Video You'll Ever See"—I was even deliberately brash. I sent emails to the big conservative think tanks, explaining my project and asking for their best arguments. I asked for help in some climate skeptic discussion groups. I even contacted economist Ross McKitrick, the most prestigious economic expert on the skeptical side. I figured if he didn't know, nobody did.

I'm usually quite civil. It felt kind of naughty!

This chapter is a result of that search. You will probably find different sources from the ones I found. That is, after all, part of the point of this whole book—for you to go through your own process of discovery to arrive at your own conclusion, without having to rely on believing me.

Recall that a wide variety of viewpoints get lumped into my definition of a skeptic as somebody who opposes taking significant action to cut carbon emissions. So you will find sources in here that indeed say humans are warming the globe and lower carbon emissions would be a desirable thing. But the bottom line is, this chapter lists sources that would argue that column B is the better bet in the global warming grid.

Page 102.

Professional Societies

AMERICAN ASSOCIATION OF PETROLEUM GEOLOGISTS (AAPG)

As detailed on page 90, AAPG was the last professional scientific organization to abandon its official statement skeptical of global warming, and it changed its stance in response to pressure from a significant number of its members. The original statement said that any projected climate change was natural, and that if the globe did warm, it would be beneficial to humans.

The new statement, adopted in 2007, said that the globe is warming but the membership is divided on the degree of human influence. It also acknowledged that other professional organizations state that humans are significantly changing the climate to negative effect. However, the authors pointed out that it might still be natural and that the worst-case predictions of some computer models are not necessarily true.

As a professional organization, AAPG goes at the top level of my spectrum, though an argument can be made for putting it low in that section because its members stand to lose their jobs if the economy shifts away from fossil fuels (increasing potential bias).

Think Tanks and Advocacy Organizations

COPENHAGEN CONSENSUS

Convened in 2004 by Danish political scientist Bjorn Lomborg, the Copenhagen Consensus was a temporary project made up of eight leading economists (three of which were Nobel

I'll talk more about him in a minute.

Prize winners). Its task was to prioritize the main problems facing humanity, essentially answering the question, If we want to get the biggest bang for our buck in terms of human well-being, what should we spend money on? It ranked HIV/AIDS prevention as the top priority out of its list of 17 problems, and combating climate change at the very bottom, in a category dubbed "Bad Projects."

As a sort of think tank, I would put the Copenhagen Consensus fairly high in the Big Fuzzy Middle; though only eight experts did the evaluation, three of them were Nobel laureates.

FRASER INSTITUTE'S "INDEPENDENT SUMMARY FOR POLICYMAKERS" (ISPM)

The Fraser Institute is a Canadian economic think tank, whose official view of global warming emphasizes that significant uncertainties remain in climate science, though it doesn't explicitly deny that humans are warming the planet.

The institute was critical of the IPCC's 2007 report, so it produced its own summary for policy makers. Each of the IPCC report sections included a summary of the findings, and a common criticism made by skeptics is that those summaries misrepresented the sections they were attached to because they downplayed uncertainty in the science and ignored contrary evidence. The "Independent Summary for Policymakers" (ISPM) was the Fraser Institute's attempt to set the record straight. A panel of 10 experts produced its own, more representative summary of the same IPCC report.

While the ISPM didn't say that global warming isn't a problem and we can all just relax, it did conclude that the certainty and magnitude of global warming were overstated; thus, I am categorizing it as a skeptical view, because it would seem to oppose a significant cut to emissions.

> Recall my definition of a skeptic from page 36.

I place it in the Big Fuzzy Middle of my credibility spectrum in the think tank category.

THE HEARTLAND INSTITUTE

The Heartland Institute is a major player in the popular debate, organizing the 2008 International Conference on Climate Change in New York City, a meeting of individuals skeptical of global warming. It also promotes a standing invitation to Al Gore to debate climate change with prominent skeptics. As a clearinghouse of skeptical information, its website provides a useful "PolicyBot" function, which allows you to easily search papers from think tanks and advocacy groups on the issue of climate change.

> Gore hasn't accepted yet. Busy guy, I suppose.

The Heartland Institute's mission, as given on its website, is "to discover and promote free-market solutions to social and economic problems." This would seem to introduce possible bias because significant cuts to emissions are generally understood to require substantial government involvement, which free-marketers are generally lukewarm about. So, while it goes at the think tank level of my spectrum, I would put the Heartland Institute low down in that level because of its potential bias on the issue (just like I would with the Sierra Club, for instance).

Recall the discussion of bias on page 80.

THE STANDARD BEARERS: THE HEAVYWEIGHT CONSERVATIVE THINK TANKS

There are a number of Washington-based conservative think tanks that are significant players in the debate. While global warming is only one of many issues that each organization focuses on, I include them here because they arguably produce most of the policy papers, speakers, and analysts that are the voice of the skeptical view in the popular debate. If you do any reading about the issue, you will soon run across a mention of at least one of them in the mainstream media.

Because they're think tanks, all go in the Big Fuzzy Middle of my credibility spectrum. All of them have potentially strong bias because of their free market/libertarian mission statements.

THE COMPETITIVE ENTERPRISE INSTITUTE (CEI)

The Competitive Enterprise Institute (CEI) frequently produces and airs TV ads touting a skeptical attitude toward global warming, including a now-infamous 2006 spot that virtually sings the praises of having more CO_2 in the air (because plants need it), complete with pretty piano music, slow-motion footage of kids blowing dandelions, and the breathy tagline: "Carbon dioxide—they call it pollution. We call it life."

THE CATO INSTITUTE

While Cato's strict libertarian philosophy has put it at odds with other conservative think tanks over issues like immigration and legalization of marijuana (it favors both), its fundamental philosophy opposing government control puts it shoulder-to-shoulder with the others on global warming.

THE HERITAGE FOUNDATION

In my search for economic disaster scenarios, I found a
1998 paper from Heritage warning of "devastating economic
consequences" if the United States adopted the Kyoto Protocol
for limiting greenhouse gas emissions. The paper was based
on the 1998 Energy Information Administration (EIA) report,
calling that report "the knockout punch." But the most devastating consequence it could pull out of that report was a
worst-case projection of gas prices as high as $1.91 per
gallon by 2010. For me, a black mark like that discredits any
future predictions of economic doom it might make.

Page 128.

Page 147.

THE MARSHALL INSTITUTE

According to the research of Naomi Oreskes, the Marshall Institute is at the center of the alleged disinformation campaign about climate change. While its online
statement about climate change is surprisingly warmer-ish
("There is a sufficient basis for action because the climate
change risk is real"), the institute's publications are exclusively
(and strongly) skeptical.

Page 126.

Petitions and Other Self-Selecting Statements

THE OREGON PETITION

Written in 1999 to oppose the Kyoto Protocol, the Oregon Petition has had substantial influence; Nebraska senator Chuck
Hagel even held up a copy on the Senate floor during a debate
on a global warming treaty. It's morphed through several
names, so if you come across any references to "a petition of
31,000 [19,000, 17,000] scientists," "The Petition Project," "the
Oregon Petition," or "The Global Warming Petition," remember that they all refer to this document.

It states that there is "no convincing scientific evidence" that humans may disrupt the climate. It also asserts that limiting emissions would actually harm humans and the environment, and that increases in CO_2 levels will actually be beneficial.

It suffers from several factors that significantly reduce its credibility for me. First, it was promoted with materials so well designed to look like they'd come from the National Academy of Sciences that the real NAS was forced to reassert its position on global warming in response to press inquires about why it had suddenly reversed its position.

Second, the Oregon Petition suffered from poor quality control over who got to sign it, and the organizers took off bogus names (including characters from the TV series *M*A*S*H*) only after the signatures were publicly ridiculed by warmers. And even if you wanted to make your own evaluation of the credibility of the signers, you wouldn't be able to because their affiliations are not listed, so it's impossible to look up the background of anyone.

So, despite its impressive number of signatures, this petition has almost no credibility for me. But because I haven't established any way to demote something *down* out of the Big Fuzzy Middle of my credibility spectrum (and shouldn't do so now because that would seem to be a screaming example of confirmation bias), I will limit myself to putting this petition at the very bottom of that section.

"U.S. SENATE REPORT: OVER 400 PROMINENT SCIENTISTS DISPUTED MAN-MADE GLOBAL WARMING CLAIMS IN 2007"

The "U. S. Senate Report: Over 400 Prominent Scientists Disputed Man-Made Global Warming Claims in 2007" is popularly referred to as "a list of 400 scientists against global warming." This sounds authoritative on the face of it, but because the document has multiple strikes against it, I don't give it much credibility.

It's packaged as an official Senate report, complete with the official Senate seal on the cover, but a closer look reveals it is just a paper put together by a member of Senator Inhofe's staff. That seems intentionally deceptive to me.

It also does a lot of double counting. I stumbled across one individual who had been counted *three* times—once as an individual, once as a signer of a letter to the United Nations from more than 100 "prominent international scientists," and once as a signer of a letter to the Canadian prime minister from 60 "prominent scientists."

It's hard not to have a name like Zbiqniew jump out at you as you scroll by. Gesundheit?

The title refers to "scientists," but many of the individuals mentioned are not scientists at all but engineers, inventors, economists, and so on. And many of them don't dispute global warming—like the title claims—but merely say the issue needs further study to reduce the remaining uncertainty.

But make your own judgment when you look at it.

All these factors seriously damage the report's credibility for me, so I place it low down in the Big Fuzzy Middle.

THE MANHATTAN DECLARATION

The Manhattan Declaration is a petition that grew out of the Heartland Institute's 2008 International Conference on Climate Change. Signed by more than 500 endorsers, the declaration states that there is no convincing evidence that carbon emissions change the climate, that attempts to curb emissions will "pointlessly curtail" prosperity, and that all policies that attempt to curtail emissions should be abandoned immediately.

It's not clear how many of the signers have qualifications

to evaluate the science or economics of climate change. Because it's a petition, I put the declaration in the Big Fuzzy Middle of my spectrum.

I got bogged down for several hours trying to figure it out and then remembered my own advice—the last item in the Checklist of Equipment on page 105! It is so hard to keep from getting sucked in to the details.

NONGOVERNMENTAL INTERNATIONAL PANEL ON CLIMATE CHANGE (NIPCC)

Page 139.

Headed by atmospheric physicist S. Fred Singer, the Nongovernmental International Panel on Climate Change (NIPCC), made up of 23 people, is similar in purpose to the "Independent Summary for Policymakers" I discussed earlier. The panel has provided its own summary of the IPCC report to balance the latter's politically motivated statements.

In the introduction to the document, we find the bottom line:

Page 130.

> Before undergoing a major operation, wouldn't you seek a "second opinion"? When a nation faces an important decision that risks its economic future, or perhaps the fate of the ecology, it should do the same. It is a time-honored tradition to set up a "Team B," which examines the same original evidence but may reach a different conclusion.

The panel does indeed reach a different conclusion—that natural causes dominate climate change.

Because this document is similar to a petition—it was put together by individuals who came together for a couple workshops—I place the NIPCC's document in the Big Fuzzy Middle of my spectrum.

THE LEIPZIG DECLARATION

I have a little confession to make. When my initial research into the Leipzig Declaration turned up a rat's nest of different versions and a swarm of controversies, and I saw that it was linked to several sources that I'd already decided had low credibility, I stopped looking and didn't bother to look up the backgrounds of the signers. I'm not made of time.

I share this with you (rather than shamefully hiding it) because I realize it presents a useful lesson. If we insist on being perfect in our evaluation of the issue, then most of us (myself included) will never even get off the couch to get to the better-than-nothing level. Part of the strength of the credibility spectrum and the decision grid is that they don't require perfection. You do what you can with the time you've got, make a provisional decision, and then remain open to new information.

I placed the Leipzig Declaration low in the Big Fuzzy Middle. But if, in the end, my dressed credibility spectrum doesn't give a clear indication of likelihood and consequence, then I can come back and look into this declaration more closely to see if it's any sort of tiebreaker.

Individual Professionals (Scientists and Economists)

RICHARD LINDZEN

Richard Lindzen is the most prominent scientist among the skeptics. He is a climatologist at the Massachusetts Institute of Technology and a member of the National Academy of Sciences, no small feat.

Over the years he has written skeptical articles many times in influential places like the *Wall Street Journal*. His basic message is that the widespread agreement in the scientific community is a result of a "bandwagon" mentality and a search for notoriety and money. Recently, his charges have gotten more pointed, claiming in an online (non-peer-reviewed) paper in 2008 that the National Academy of Sciences and other professional organizations have been infiltrated and corrupted by environmental activists, who have influenced the statements such organizations make.

Recall Lindzen's dissent on page 90.

As far as the science, he has predicted that cooling will be just as likely as warming, that humans can't be linked to climate change, and that even if the predictions of the computer climate models were true, we wouldn't see catastrophic consequences but would in fact have fewer storms. When evaluating the credibility of these statements, I noted that all were public statements made in opinion pieces, not findings from any of Lindzen's peer-reviewed articles.

As a well-published climatologist and member of the NAS, he would normally go relatively high in the individual professional category of my spectrum. But given that his skeptical statements in this debate have been in the press and not in peer-reviewed articles, I'm not going to place him as high as Hansen, because Hansen's peer-reviewed work mirrors his public statements.

Page 125.

ROSS MCKITRICK

Ross McKitrick is a professor of economics who worked with mining consultant Steve McIntyre in successfully identifying errors in the methods used to produce the infamous hockey stick graph used in the IPCC's 2001 report, though that graph's conclusions were later confirmed by the National Research Council of the NAS. (Right answer, wrong method, essentially.)

Page 141.

McKitrick has long been an outspoken opponent of the Kyoto Protocol, producing numerous op-ed pieces and the 2002 book *Taken by Storm: The Troubled Science, Policy, and Politics of Global Warming*. He also coordinated the Fraser Institute's "Independent Summary for Policymakers," and is known for challenging the notion that "global average temperature" has a physical meaning.

Page 130.

As far as expertise, he is well qualified to speak on the economics of climate change, though his association with the libertarian Fraser Institute (where he is a senior fellow) and his characterization of warmers as "alarmists" might affect one's assessment of the bias factor when assessing his credibility. I place him at the individual professional level on my spectrum.

S. FRED SINGER

S. Fred Singer is an accomplished atmospheric physicist, who has a long résumé listing government, academic, and think tank positions. He

> He invented some of the first instruments used on weather satellites.

has been active as a skeptic in the debate from the start, and most recently co-authored the book *Unstoppable Global Warming: Every 1,500 Years*. Singer also runs the Science and Environmental Policy Project, which is a clearinghouse of skeptical sources and arguments.

The warmers love to connect Singer to the tobacco industry, accusing him of running a "campaign of disinformation" about global warming similar to what big tobacco did with the links between

> See Oreskes, page 126.

tobacco and cancer. But he is an atmospheric scientist, so I place him at the individual professional level in my spectrum.

ROBERT M. CARTER

Robert Carter is a well-published paleontologist, a founding member of the New Zealand Climate Science Coalition, and a regular contributor to the popular press on global warming. In 2007, he gave a very accessible lecture titled "Testing the Hypothesis of Dangerous Global Warming," which has made the rounds online as a video with the name "Climate Change—Is CO_2 the Cause?" In the video he "tests the hypothesis" of human-caused global warming (involving lots of graphs and data for the viewer) and finds that it fails, although at the time of this writing Carter has not published his case in a peer-reviewed journal.

I would place him at the individual professional level of my spectrum.

JOHN CHRISTY

John Christy is an accomplished atmospheric scientist and was a lead author for the IPCC's 2001 report. He and Roy Spencer (introduced next) developed a global temperature data set that earned the researchers NASA's Medal for Exceptional Scientific Achievement in 1991.

Based largely on the disagreement between his temperature record and what climate models predict, Christy is doubtful that human-made carbon emissions have any discernible effect on the climate, and if they do, it could very well be beneficial on balance, with increased food production and fewer cold-related deaths.

In 2005, Christy acknowledged errors in his data set that reduced its disagreement with climate models, but he still maintains his view that humans are not a significant factor in global warming.

His earlier accolades would normally put him high in the individual professional level, but for me, that is seriously overshadowed by the fact that he reaffirmed his beliefs rather than modified them when the evidence they were based on (the disagreement between his temperature set and the climate models) was compromised. That would seem to suggest significant bias. So I placed Christy low in that level of my spectrum.

ROY SPENCER

Roy Spencer is a research meteorologist whose work with John Christy earned NASA's Medal for Exceptional Scientific Achievement in 1991. He believes the globe is warming, but that it is primarily a natural phenomenon with minimal impact from humans, testifying to Congress: "I predict that in the coming years, there will be a growing realization among the global warming research community that most of the climate change we have observed is natural, and that mankind's role is relatively minor."

In 2008, Spencer published the bestselling book *Climate Confusion: How Global Warming Hysteria Leads to Bad Science, Pandering Politicians and Misguided Policies That Hurt the Poor*. For the same reasons I noted for Christy, I place Spencer low in the individual professional level of my spectrum.

Individual Lay People

STEVE MCINTYRE

Steve McIntyre, a mining industry consultant, is the David facing the Goliath of the climate science establishment. McIntyre and Ross McKitrick (introduced earlier) run the skeptics' website ClimateAudit.org, which is dedicated to being a watchdog of the temperature data sets that are at the heart of climate science.

McIntyre clearly knows quite a bit about what he's doing because he pointed out an error in a NASA data set that no one else had caught and that NASA subsequently acknowledged and corrected. He was also involved in the hockey stick controversy; he and McKitrick won a significant battle but lost the war.

Page 138.

While McIntyre enjoys a bit of a hero status among those who argue human-caused global warming isn't true, his own view doesn't seem to go that far. On his website, he specifically says that he doesn't claim that his work disproves global warming, only that he is concerned that the hockey stick graph that was used by the 2001 IPCC report is invalid because of how it was produced.

While McIntyre has no formal training in climate science

or economics, his success at finding errors in the NASA data set and methodology of the hockey stick graph gives him some "street cred" in my book, so I'm promoting him from the individual lay person level to just below the individual professional level.

BJORN LOMBORG

Bjorn Lomborg is perhaps the most famous figure in the global warming debate today. He is the author of two bestselling and controversial books, *The Skeptical Environmentalist: Measuring the Real State of the World* and *Cool It: The Skeptical Environmentalist's Guide to Global Warming*. He holds a PhD in political science and has taught business and statistics courses at universities in his native Denmark since 1994. I classify him as a skeptic because while he makes it clear that he believes human-caused global warming is indeed a problem, he feels it has been blown out of proportion, and he strongly opposes attempts to aggressively cut carbon emissions.

He detailed his reasoning in *Cool It* and pretty much echoed the methods and conclusions of the Copenhagen Consensus, which he convened in 2004. He argued Page 130. that the effects of global warming won't be that bad and that spending massive amounts of money to mitigate it would buy us only tiny improvements in our quality of life.

Instead, he emphasized the need to make sure our economy grows quickly enough that we can afford to adapt to the changes, such as by buying air conditioners and building levees to hold back rising seas. He does advocate cuts to carbon emissions (a 10 percent reduction by 2100), but because this reduction isn't significant, I categorize him as a skeptic.

"Simply put," he writes, "we're being force-fed vastly overhyped scare stories. . . . If we manage to stay cool, we will likely leave the twenty-first century with societies much stronger, without rampant death, suffering, and loss, and with nations much richer, with unimaginable opportunity in a cleaner, healthy environment."

Despite being neither a scientist nor an economist, I don't place Lomborg all the way down in individual lay person on my credibility spectrum because he's done way more homework than the rest of us. It is significant to me that the well-respected magazine *Scientific American* published a detailed critique of Lomborg's assertions, written by climate scientists. So I'll put him between lay person and professional.

> It's interesting to contrast this view with that of Hansen (page 125). Part of the stark difference is because Hansen bases his views on 2008 science and Lomborg bases his on the middle scenario of the 2001 IPCC report. It also bears on credibility that Hansen is a climatologist, and Lomborg is in the political and economic fields.

MARTIN DURKIN AND THE GREAT GLOBAL WARMING SWINDLE

The Great Global Warming Swindle, from British filmmaker Martin Durkin, spread explosively online when it came out in 2007 because it was seen as the skeptic's antidote to Al Gore's 2006 *An Inconvenient Truth*. Durkin used lots of graphs and interviewed scientists to assert that human-caused global warming is not true. Like Gore's movie, there has been so much bitter debate around it that I don't think it's very useful to use in my analysis. I am including it here only because it has gotten so much attention, and it's interesting to see where it fits in the big picture.

As with *An Inconvenient Truth*, I'd promote Durkin's movie from the individual lay person level because it takes a lot of research to make a documentary. However, due to the number of complaints from scientists who were involved but later claimed that their work or interviews had been distorted, I wouldn't put Durkin as high as Gore.

MICHAEL CRICHTON

The author of many popular science fiction stories, Michael Crichton wrote a 2004 bestselling novel titled *State of Fear*. While a work of fiction, the novel contained many graphs and footnotes and made the case that the current understanding of the science is too uncertain to form any reasonable conclusions, and that scientists often play up threats to ensure funding for their research.

While he had no formal scientific training (he held an MD), he did testify before Congress on global warming, and President Bush met with him for an hour to discuss the issue in 2006. Also in 2006, Crichton received the American Association of Petroleum Geologists' annual journalism award. These facts would seem to justify putting him relatively high in the individual lay person level of my credibility spectrum.

He was invited by Senator James Inhofe (page 146).

STEVE MILLOY

Steve Milloy runs the popular skeptical website JunkScience .com, which has garnered some notable mentions (including being a "hot pick" in the NetWatch feature of *Science* magazine in 1998). The site serves as a clearinghouse for the most common skeptical arguments, with features such as "Top 10 Climate Mythbusters for 2007."

His biggest splash was issuing the Ultimate Global Warming Challenge, which offers $500,000 "to the first person to prove, in a scientific manner, that humans are causing harmful global warming." No one has done so to his satisfaction, though entry details are available on his site if you want to take a stab.

Although you've got to appreciate someone who puts his money where his mouth is, the fact that Milloy has a law degree and no scientific training means I put him at the individual lay person level on my spectrum.

BENNY PEISER

Benny Peiser is a social anthropologist who made a name for himself in the global warming debate when he attempted to reproduce the survey of peer-reviewed literature on climate change that Naomi Oreskes had performed and got different results. His results indicated a greater amount of dissent in the peer-reviewed literature and were thus used to counter claims that there was consensus among scientists that Page 126. human-caused global warming was real. A mess of back-and-forth controversy ensued, and Peiser eventually retracted his results because he had made significant errors in his method.

Despite being an academic, his lack of training in science leaves him at the individual lay person level on my spectrum, and I place him low there because of his 0 for 1 track record in the subject.

LORD CHRISTOPHER WALTER, THIRD VISCOUNT MONCKTON OF BRENCHLEY

Christopher Monckton is a British business consultant (and former adviser in Margaret Thatcher's administration) who is prolific in his skepticism of global warming, and you will likely run across something from him eventually. He is a controversial figure and has been a spirited critic of the IPCC report and the Stern Review. His highest-profile contributions to Page 122. the debate include the following:

- Funding the distribution of *The Great Global Warming Swindle* to British schools.
- Giving a Gore-style lecture debunking global warming, which was filmed and distributed under the title *Apocalypse? No!*
- Writing a (non-peer-reviewed) paper in a newsletter of the American Physical Society (APS), which caused quite the brouhaha because it was interpreted by casual observers as APS reversing its official warmer state-

ment on climate change. The newsletter put a disclaimer above Monckton's paper, the arm of the APS that governs the newsletter disavowed the newsletter, and the APS itself reaffirmed its own unchanged position. What a stir!

Monckton has no scientific or economic training and is accorded only scorn by scientists as far as I can tell, so he goes low in the individual lay person level.

SENATOR JAMES INHOFE

Republican Senator James Inhofe is a very powerful and controversial figure in the popular debate on global warming. His Senate office maintains a website that is a gold mine of skeptical views, often focusing on debunking the claim that there is a consensus among scientists on the issue.

Inhofe's views and activities are too numerous to detail here, but they are all pretty much wrapped up in his most famous statement, made while he was the chair of the Senate Committee on Environment and Public Works: "Global warming is the greatest hoax ever perpetrated on the American people." Inhofe also organized the List of 400 Scientists, which I talked about earlier in this chapter.

> See Inhofe's Senate website and his Wikipedia entry for good summaries.

I place Senator Inhofe at the individual lay person level of my credibility spectrum. His track record: For years he has announced that the tide of scientific opinion has shifted to the skeptical side, without yet being vindicated; he doesn't have much credibility with me.

> I base this judgment on the statements from the professional societies listed in Chapter 6.

Economic Sources

The statements I examined from economic sources don't argue for a position in the global warming debate. However, the skeptical argument usually boils down to the claim that taking action would cost too much, and these statements detail costs, so this chapter seemed a more appropriate place to include them than the warmer's chapter.

On my credibility spectrum, I put economic sources on the line halfway between the warmers and skeptics, just to remind myself to take them into account when I'm estimating the contents of the boxes on my decision grid. I put the Stern Review on the warmers' side because it concluded that the costs of inaction are greater than the costs of action, which would support the argument for column A.

I was looking for sources that might substantiate the worst-case scenario I put into the top left of the decision grid, such as a major depression triggered by the action taken to significantly reduce carbon emissions. But I couldn't find anything that described a scenario like that—all I found was a bunch of econometric numbers that I don't know how to interpret.

So I pulled out the two numbers that most of us are familiar with: gasoline prices and gross domestic product (GDP; a measure of economic growth).

ENERGY INFORMATION ADMINISTRATION (EIA)

A 1998 report titled "Impacts of the Kyoto Protocol on U.S. Energy Markets and Economic Activity" gives a worst-case scenario of gasoline prices rising as high as $1.91 a gallon by 2010 and the GDP shrinking by 4 percent over the course of 4 years (2008 to 2012).

The report was issued by the Energy Information Administration of the U.S. Department of Energy, so it goes at the government report level.

ANALYSIS AND MODELING GROUP (AMG)

In 2000, the Analysis and Modeling Group (AMG) of the Canadian government released a report titled "An Assessment of the Economic and Environmental Implications for Canada of the Kyoto Protocol."

The worst-case scenario I found was a possible reduction in GDP of 3 percent over a decade: "It is important to provide perspective on these estimates. For example, a reduction in GDP of 3 percent in 2010 means that, over the decade, the economy will grow by about 26 percent instead of 30 percent as projected in the reference case."

As a government report, I'd put this fairly high on my spectrum, again on the line between the two sides.

CHAPTER 8

IT'S NOT THE TEMP THAT GETS YA: DEMYSTIFYING THE DOOMSDAY

Most people are familiar with the basics of global warming—by burning fossil fuels and cutting down trees, we are releasing carbon dioxide into the air, which then traps more of the sun's heat, raising the temperature in- side, kind of like the glass panes of a greenhouse do. Thicker panes, warmer greenhouse.

> Hence the term greenhouse effect.

There are many "greenhouse gases" that act like this, the most important being water, carbon dioxide (CO_2), and meth- ane. Water is the dominant gas in the greenhouse effect, but no one really talks about it because we can't do anything about how much is in the air. When people talk about carbon emis- sions, they are generally referring to CO_2, though sometimes they're lumping in methane because it's got a carbon atom in the middle, just like CO_2 does.

Greenhouse gases are a good thing. Without them we wouldn't be here. But too much of a good thing isn't necessar- ily a better thing.

Still, the shrill urgency of the warmers I talked about in Chapter 6 defies common sense. Heads of global corporations calling for government regulation of themselves? Military brass having a "We're all gonna die!" hissy fit? All from a couple degrees of warming? Just what the heck is going on here?

The skeptic's arguments seem much more level-headed: Don't rush into anything. The climate has always changed naturally—why are we suddenly the bad guys? Why threaten the economy when we're not even sure there's a problem?

Why the Warmers?

So what's up with the warmers?

That's what we'll explore in this chapter—the central arguments of the warmers. When something seems unreasonable, we naturally discount it. And the claims of many of the warmers seem very unreasonable. But, having learned a bit about the pitfalls your brain sets for you, you probably realize now that dismissing something out of hand because it seems unreasonable may not serve your best interests. After all, the history of science shows that the physical world is chockablock of things that at first seemed unreasonable but later turned out to be true.

> What do you mean the earth goes around the sun? I can see the sun moving with my own eyes, you dope!

So, to help you not be influenced by the unreasonableness of the warmer's statements as you place them on your credibility spectrum, it is worth taking a look at where these guys are coming from. I won't discuss the skeptics' arguments because those are much easier to understand: Don't risk your economy and liberties until you definitely know you have to.

Most all of what follows is well-established science, and the basic physics are universally acknowledged: Carbon dioxide traps heat in the atmosphere, human activities have released significant amounts of it in the last 150 years (most of that in the last 30 years), and levels of carbon dioxide in the atmosphere have been steadily increasing since we started measuring 50 years ago.

The debate in the scientific community lies in the question of how significant and quick any warming would be. Everyone agrees that the possibilities detailed in this chapter exist. The disagreement is about whether they will add up to not much or to the end of 90 percent of all life on the planet.

The Carbon Cycle: Is That Anthracite in Your Borehole or Are You Just Happy to See Me?

First, some basics.

Let's start with the plants. They are mind-bogglingly amazing little devices. They take in sunlight and store the energy, so that when we burn or eat them, we get the energy back out. The energy we get out of plants is actually the sun's energy that went into making them. In essence, they are solar energy storage devices. When we release that energy through burning or by digesting them, we also release CO_2 as the byproduct. Why is it CO_2 that the plants release? That part is important to our story.

Here's a shocker: Plants are made mostly of air. They breathe in carbon dioxide from the air and then use energy from the sun to rip that molecule apart into carbon and oxygen atoms. They combine the carbon with water (and a little stuff from the soil) and rearrange the atoms like Legos to build themselves (their stalks, leaves, fruits), expelling the oxygen as a waste product.

> This cheery little scenario has recently been brought to the table by paleontologist Peter Ward and others, who demonstrated that such an event—a small bump triggering runaway global warming—was probably responsible for the largest mass extinction in the earth's history (bigger than the one that killed the dinosaurs). He definitely gets the title of "Dr. Doomiest."

> Vocab: One carbon dioxide molecule is made of one carbon atom attached to two oxygen atoms.

> Ever look at an oak tree that was once a puny acorn and wonder, Where did all that stuff come from? It wasn't the soil!

So the upshot is, plants stitch themselves together from carbon in the air, using energy from the sun, and then spit out oxygen for us to breathe. How convenient for us! They make a handy, portable, yummy package of stored solar energy, with a side of oxygen. Too cool!

That's why I hug trees. Just sayin' thanks! Although, in fact, most of the planet's oxygen comes from single-celled plants in the ocean called phytoplankton (FIE-tow-plank-tun).

Over the last 300,000,000 years, when some of those plants died, they got buried. Shoved deep in the earth, their

More Legos fun!

atoms got rearranged again, turning into what we call *fossil fuels*. Coal is rearranged plants from swamps, and oil is rearranged plankton from the oceans. When we dig that stuff back up, it still contains the stored energy that the plants absorbed from the sun.

That's why oil and coal are our "magic" fuels: we just dig them up, and—because the huge amounts of energy are stored in a very stable and compact form—we can safely haul them to wherever we need the energy. Once there, we combine them with oxygen ("burn" them), which releases the energy that was

Next time you feel the warm hood of your car, that's ancient sunlight flowing into your hand. Pretty wild!

captured 300,000,000 years ago and has been stored underground since then.

And what do you get when you burn the stuff, combining the carbon from the fossil fuel with the oxygen from the air? CO_2! Which is right back where we started. But CO_2 isn't poisonous, and it's never been a problem, so we just vent it into the air and let it drift away, where it feeds the plants again, and the wheels on the bus go round and round.

So what's the big deal?

Coal, 5 pounds.

The Carbon Transfer Project— Otherwise Known as the Age of Fossil Fuels

See this bag?

It's a 5-pound sack of coal—almost pure carbon, dug up from the ground, where it's been stored for some hundreds of millions of years. The coal is full of that ancient sunlight, trapped in the chemical bonds between the carbon atoms. What's the significance of the 5-pound sack?

This is the amount of carbon that you put in the air with every gallon of gasoline you burn. If you're in a Hummer, that'll get you maybe 12 miles, and if you're in a Prius, that'll get you four times as far.

The problem is not that we're running out of fossil fuels. We will fairly soon, but that's a different book. The problem (say the

> Specifically, a book about Peak Oil—the point at which world oil production begins its final decline. We'll be able to put little upward bumps in that curve, but overall, it's downhill forevermore.

warmers) is that we've been burning so much of the stuff that the waste bin we've been using—the atmosphere—is start0ing to overflow. Not in the sense that we can't fit any more CO_2 in there, but in the sense that it's now making a difference in the way the atmosphere—and therefore our weather patterns—behaves.

That's because even though the CO_2 we're putting into the atmosphere was *originally there* to begin with, the particular carbon atom I emit from my tailpipe hasn't been in the air for a long, long time. It's all a matter of time scale. We didn't really start this huge transfer of carbon from underground into the air until the Industrial Revolution got going around 150 years ago, and within a few decades (for oil, that is—longer for coal), we'll have pretty much completed the process.

So the crux of the matter is that we are taking the carbon that has been stashed away underground over the last 300,000,000 years and burping it back into the air over the course of about 200 years. On a geologic time scale, that's a blink of an eye.

The "Right" Climate

But, you might be saying, it's probably just a few degrees of warming, right? Sometimes I feel kind of chilly. Why the warmer thrashfest?

Well, small changes can take off and turn themselves into big changes with no further help from us, through the amplifying magic of feedback mechanisms, which we'll explore in a minute. Still, maybe that would be a good thing, or at least not a catastrophic thing. Ask any Canadian if he or she would like to be a little warmer. Who's to say what the "right" climate is, anyway?

And remember where I am on the credibility spectrum: riiiiight at the top.

I am.

And I'll do it right here. The right climate is . . . the current one.

Why? Because it's the one our civilization is based on. Our cities are located on current coastlines and rivers. Our agricultural economies are based on current growing seasons and rainfall patterns. Our societies are adapted to current disease patterns. Our flood control and storm water and waste treatment facilities are designed for current rainfall patterns.

Every single human settlement is designed specifically for the climate it is currently in. The concern with climate change is that it might amount to something like spinning the wheel and swapping places with another settlement in a different climate, which wouldn't generally be a smooth transition.

Global Climate Destabilization

How can all that come from some rising temperatures? The warmers worry that our transfer of carbon from underground to the air is so big and so sudden that it will not just change the climate but *destabilize* the climate. Big, rapid changes to complicated systems are rarely smooth and orderly. That's why as time goes on, you'll probably come to hear less of the term climate *change* and more of the terms climate *destabilization*, climate *disruption*, and climate *crisis*. For the more poetically inclined, there's always climate *chaos* and global *weirding*.

What might that look like? Here are some of the feasible scenarios that have the worrywarts up at night. Several of these changes have been observed already, although it cannot be said that global warming "caused" any single event. Global warming just changes the odds, so I present these phenomena here not as evidence that climate change has started but as a sort of preview of what the warmers are worried about. Their concern is that these events could become the norm in a destabilized climate.

- Rising *sea levels* not only take over coastline real estate, pushing people inland, but also increase storm surges, which are the main cause of property damage from hurricanes. As sea levels get high enough, they start to break into the water treatment systems of metropolitan areas, leading to compromised public health and more disease.

- The ranges of *pest populations* expand, increasing crop losses. History is littered with examples of how a non-native organism introduced into a new ecosystem can become invasive and run rampant—think kudzu, nutria, starlings, and Africanized bees. The migration of pest populations with changing regional climates could naturally bring about the same dynamic.

- The range of *disease-spreading insects* expands, bringing increases in deadly diseases, such as malaria.

- *Rainfall patterns* change. More concentrated rains lead to flooding and topsoil loss. Warmer temperatures mean less precipitation falls as snow, reducing the snowpack that feeds watersheds during the summer, causing frequent droughts.

- More frequent or more severe *extreme weather* events, such as hurricanes, tornados, and ice storms.

- A collapse of the *ocean conveyor belt* would probably result in Europe getting colder. Page 166. Northern Europe is at the same latitude as Siberia but is kept temperate by the ocean currents bringing warm water up from the tropics.

- As *regional climates* migrate northward, a forest ends up in a climate that stresses it out, increasing its susceptibility to disease and allowing more insect attacks. Eventually a significant part of the forest may die. *Dead forest* is just another term

This has already been observed in western Canada, where a forest the size of England has been killed by an infestation of pine beetles.

for "huge tinderbox," and it's just a matter of time before a lightning strike sets off a massive wildfire. Once burned, the forest won't regenerate well because the seeds are in the wrong climate.

- As the climate changes, relationships among *fungi, parasites,* and *beneficial insects* may change rapidly, causing wide-ranging effects on agriculture and our food supply.

All events such as these would put pressure on already weak systems and countries, possibly pushing them over the brink into resource wars, failed states, increased terrorism, and waves of environmental refugees. It gives you an idea of why the national security sources mentioned in Chapter 6 consider potential climate destabilization to be a national security threat.

The explosive spread of Colony Collapse Disorder in U.S. honeybee populations in 2006 highlighted how dependent our agriculture is on commercial beehives for pollination ($15 billion a year) and how fragile that agricultural system may be.

Remember that deceptively dry line from the Pentagon report? "With inadequate preparation, the result could be a significant drop in the human carrying capacity of the Earth's environment."

Feedback Fun and Complex Systems

So the bottom line is this: It's not the temperature rise that gets you but what it causes. Like it's not the bullet that kills you but the blood loss and organ failure. A bullet is just a piece of metal, and we use bits of metal all the time without any harm. But what that metal ends up pushing against—and how fast it does so—makes all the difference.

That's why focusing on the temperature change misses the point. What really matters is how a small but sudden change in the temperature might throw a monkey wrench in the whole climate system. And, as we'll see, it may not require something as violent as a bullet. For instance, a light tap on the

There are a number of terms that refer to such systems, such as <u>chaotic system</u> and <u>nonlinear dynamical system,</u> and various combinations and shortened forms of those. For readability, I will refer to these simply as complex systems or nonlinear systems.

chest might not seem threatening. Unless you happen to be balanced on top of a post.

The warmers worry that the slight tap we're giving to the climate might spell doomsday because the climate is what's called a *complex dynamical system*. I will grossly oversimplify the concept by describing such a system as something with lots of little bits that are highly interconnected to each other, including ones that are connected back to *themselves*.

You'll probably recall the nerve-wracking times on Wall Street in the fall of 2008—"the week that broke Wall Street" and such. That happened so suddenly because the stock market is a complex system, capable of unexpected lurches owing to the bits that are connected back to themselves.

Such bits are called *feedback mechanisms*. Just like the feedback caused by putting a microphone in front of its own amplifier—the microphone *feeds* the output of the speaker *back* into the speaker, and you end up with a huge screech started by just a small sound. Feedback mechanisms are what can allow a minor disturbance to rock the whole system.

One feedback mechanism in the stock market is the share price of a stock: Lots of selling makes stock prices go down, which makes a bunch of nervous shareholders sell, which depresses the price further, triggering even further selling, and you're off to the races. As you may recall, a triggered feedback loop can be . . . startling.

But why doesn't a price drop trigger that loop all the time? Because there are other feedback loops that act against that. For instance, lower prices can mean a more attractive buy, which increases demand, which puts upward pressure back on the falling prices. The net result of these two types of feedback depends on how the two forces balance out at any given time, and as we saw in the week that broke Wall Street, sometimes the bottom can abruptly fall out.

"Positive" feedback amplifies changes, and "negative" feedback dampens them.

That's part of why the meltdown of the financial system in 2008 was so stunning to so many of us. We thought we had a handle on how the stock market behaves, and we knew it could be volatile, but complex systems have surprisingly huge and abrupt lurches hidden within—you can predict trends but not events. Unfortunately, we were in the test tube, and the cost of that lesson was pretty high.

That's part of what has so many of the fuddy-duddies all wound up about climate change. The global climate is way more complex than the financial system, and this time the test tube in which we're running the experiment isn't just the economy—it's the planet. (Economy included.) If we end up learning a similar lesson about the unexpected behavior of the climate system, the lesson may not do us any good. No do-overs when you've only got one planet.

Let's Take a Bath

But if you've tried to understand the specifics of the doomsday reasoning, you've probably run into the same confusing babble of terms I have. For instance, when asked what the target for taking action should be, you'll hear the *same* egghead say "350 parts per million" in one statement, "1.8°F" in another, and "cut emissions 80 percent by 2050" in yet a third. It's like switching back and forth between metric and standard measurements in the middle of a sentence—fine for the brainiacs, but it leaves the rest of us with a headache and an urge to reach for the remote.

To understand how specific feedback mechanisms in the climate might translate a relatively small temperature rise into total destabilization, we need to look a little more closely at how the climate works. Our journey starts in the bathtub.

Imagine the planet's atmosphere as a bathtub, with carbon dioxide as the water. This is, of course, tremendously oversimplified (I drew a bathtub, for Pete's sake!), but it's a good starting point for understanding the bottom line.

There is a drain at the bottom taking water out at the same time that the spigot is putting water in. If the spigot is running *faster* than the drain, then over time the water level creeps up. If the spigot is running *slower* than the drain, then the water level creeps down. If those two are equal, then the water level stays constant.

The handle on the spigot determines how fast the water flows in, and we can control that. If the inflow and outflow of water are both constant, then the water level creeps up or down at a constant pace. But if we slowly crank open the handle—even at a steady speed—the rise in water level *accelerates*, because the water flows into the tub faster and faster as time goes on.

If, at the same time, the drain gets progressively more clogged and flows slower, the accelerating water level rise will accelerate even more. If we really want to see some zooming, instead of just cranking the handle open at a steady speed, we can crank it open faster and faster. (This is the current situation—more in a moment.)

It we want to stabilize the water level (stop the rise and keep it at a steady level), not only do we need to quit spinning the handle farther and farther open but we have to actually crank it *back down* until the inflow again matches the outflow. If we're really in a hurry to stabilize the water level, we can ream out the drain at the same time to speed up the outflow.

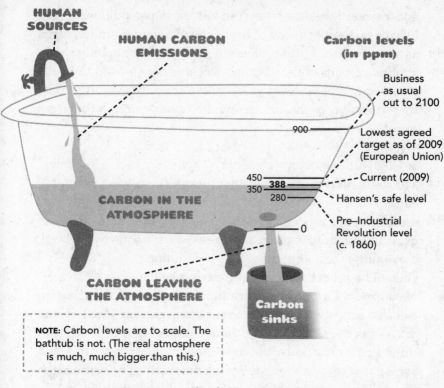

HUMAN
SOURCES

HUMAN CARBON
EMISSIONS

Carbon levels
(in ppm)

Business
as usual
out to 2100

900

Lowest agreed
target as of 2009
(European Union)

450
388
350
280

Current (2009)

Hansen's safe level

0

Pre–Industrial
Revolution level
(c. 1860)

CARBON IN THE
ATMOSPHERE

CARBON LEAVING
THE ATMOSPHERE

Carbon
sinks

NOTE: Carbon levels are to scale. The
bathtub is not. (The real atmosphere
is much, much bigger than this.)

The planetary bathtub.

Feel clean and refreshed? Now let's get down and dirty again with the techno-talk and look at the bathtub model as it applies to climate change.

CARBON LEVELS

The water is carbon dioxide in the atmosphere, and the level in the tub is referred to as *carbon levels* or *atmospheric concentration of carbon,* which just means how much of the stuff is in the air. Higher carbon levels mean a higher average global temperature, which of course is the thing that drives this whole debate. At the start of the Industrial Revolution about 150 years ago, carbon levels were around 280 parts per million (ppm). (That's just a fancy way of saying "0.028 percent of the air is carbon dioxide.") It's now around 388 ppm and not only rising at about 2 ppm every year but accelerating (it used to be increasing at 1 ppm every year) due to the exponential growth that governs both our economic model and population growth.

CARBON SINKS

The drain represents things that "uptake" carbon from the atmosphere—like CO_2 dissolving in the ocean and being used by growing phytoplankton and trees—and these things are sometimes called carbon sinks. The process is known as *carbon se-*

That's carbon <u>see-kweh-STRAY-shun</u>. But don't worry about the pronunciation. I still trip over it.

questration. Carbon sequestration is a natural process, but we can also actively do things that sequester carbon. Planting lots of trees is the simplest way, though as the debate develops, I think you'll hear more and more about aggressive, high-tech ways to make it happen—injecting pressurized CO_2 under the ground, charring and burying trees, fertilizing phytoplankton, and so on.

CARBON EMISSIONS

The spigot represents human activities (mainly burning fossil fuels) that add carbon dioxide to the atmosphere, and we control the handle. The inflow stream from the spigot is the *annual carbon emissions*—how much carbon we transfer from the ground to the air every year—and it's measured in gigatons of carbon per year (GtC/yr).

When I started following this stuff in the early 1990s, global carbon emissions were about 6 GtC/yr. In 2009, they're about 10 GtC/yr. The exponential growth of the global economy and population is what spins the handle open faster and faster—this is what's meant by such statements as, "Carbon emissions are growing by 3 percent per year" (because the inflow is growing). As I mentioned earlier, this is the current state of affairs.

In the 1990s, emissions were growing by 1 percent per year. So the increase _itself_ is increasing. Whoa. I'm getting a little dizzy here.

There are other huge flows in and out of the tub from natural processes, but they balance each other out, so I'm not including them in the picture. For instance, you'll sometimes hear that "The oceans emit 10 times as much CO_2 as humans." But they also absorb that same amount, so there's no net effect on carbon levels.

I will point out a source of confusion. Unfortunately, the amount of water in the tub (concentration of atmospheric carbon) and the amount of water flowing in every year (carbon emissions) are usually given in two different units of measurement: ppm for the former and GtC for the latter. So you can't just add last year's emissions to last year's carbon level to come up with the current carbon level. It bugs me to no end, but that's just the way it is.

It can be done, but not without lots of algebra and a headache.

CONTROLLING CARBON

Continuing with business as usual (fossil fuels, steady economic growth, typical population growth) would put carbon levels around 900 ppm in the year 2100. Looking at the marks on the side of the tub, that doesn't seem reasonable. It's taken us 150 years to get from 280 ppm to the current 388 ppm—how could we cover the remaining distance in just the next 90 years?

As I noted, business as usual—which is based on the exponential growth that governs both our economic model and population growth—means that the spigot handle is not only being continually turned open but is actually being opened _faster and faster_. Combine that with a drain that is getting smaller (due to loss of forests, reduced CO_2 solubility in the oceans, reduced upwelling of nutrients for the phytoplankton—all described later in the chapter), and it no longer seems unreasonable that the water level in our tub is expected to zoom upward at a breathtaking rate over the coming decades.

And you might get a sense of some of the warmers' agitation when it's pointed out that the last time carbon levels in the atmosphere were above even 500 ppm was about 30 million years ago.

So let's say you're a warmer, and you are nervous about the water level in the tub getting too high. What are your options? You can't get out—this is the only tub around, and you need to be in one. So you try to get the spinning of the handle to stop speeding up and instead just spin farther open at a steady rate. (This is tough, because it's run by committee.) Then you try to clean out the drain to get it to flow faster. Then you go back to the handle, which is still spinning farther open (though no longer speeding up, thank goodness), and try to actually *slow down* the spinning.

You succeed in slowing it down and through great effort manage not only to stop the spinning altogether but to crank it *back down* a bit so that the water flowing into the tub again matches the water flowing out, and the level stabilizes, or holds steady (although at it's highest level in millions of years). So can you finally relax?

> See page 237 for a translation into bathtub terms the phrases you'll hear in the public debate. Although cutting emissions and cutting the growth of emissions sound the same, the concepts are worlds apart.

> Geez, this is a high-strung bunch. Will they _ever_ be happy?

No, say the warmers. Because they've discovered something new that's *really* got them in a panic. And to understand what that is, read on.

Your Friendly Climate

We've already seen that the climate is a complex system and that positive feedback loops in such systems can spring huge, unexpected changes on you. To understand why some of the warmers might be almost hysterical with dread, it helps to know some of the specific feedback mechanisms in the global climate. All of these are fed by increased CO_2 in the air, and they eventually put more CO_2 into the air, feeding themselves.

THE WORLD'S SMALLEST PLANTS

Near the surface of the ocean, the phytoplankton—just like land plants—take in huge amounts of CO_2 from the air, keeping the carbon to build their little bodies. If the surface of the ocean warms up a little bit, that decreases the upwelling that brings nutrients from the depths, which leads to fewer growing phytoplankton. Fewer phytoplankton means less CO_2 is removed from the air, and off you go in the feedback loop.

HUG A TREE

Forests can give rise to the same feedback mechanism as the phytoplankton do. As we saw, migrating climates can lead to suddenly dead Page 156. forests, which can then turn into suddenly massive wildfires. Not only do you lose your forest but you lose a huge carbon sink.

But to add insult to injury, when all that wood burns, it releases back into the atmosphere all the carbon that used to make up the trees. So not only does the forest stop taking carbon *out* of the air but it emits carbon *into* the air. This is the double whammy that's got the Carbonistas all up in arms about clearing and burning rain-forest land.

THE ALBEDO EFFECT

Shiny white ice sheets reflect sunlight. (That's what the word *albedo* in the albedo effect means—how much something reflects the sunlight back into space.) When the temperature goes up you lose a little ice, so less sunlight is reflected and more is absorbed by the darker rock or water underneath. This increases the temperature, and you loop back around, accelerating the process.

THE METHANE GUN

Methane is a way more powerful greenhouse gas than CO_2. And a huge amount of methane is trapped at the bottom of the ocean in the form of "hydrates," kind of frozen together with water. Increasing the water temperature melts a little of the methane hydrates, which end up in the air, and there you go.

You'll also hear them referred to as <u>methane clathrates</u>, though you're on your own for pronouncing that.

There's some decent evidence that in the past this feedback process hit a point at which it suddenly all went off. This is what's sometimes referred to as the *methane gun*, and it probably played a significant role in at least one of the mass extinction events in the distant past.

STOP THE CONVEYER! I WANT TO GET OFF!

Carbon from the atmosphere ends up in the surface water of the ocean (both as dissolved CO_2 and as part of the bodies of the plankton). The ocean conveyor belt carries the surface water down to the bottom of the ocean in the North Atlantic, effectively sequestering the carbon.

Warmer temperatures melt more ice on land, increasing the flow of freshwater into the North Atlantic and slowing down the conveyor belt because freshwater doesn't sink as well. A slower ocean conveyor sequesters less carbon, allowing more of our emissions to build up in the atmosphere, increasing temperature, and on and on. This is part of why you'll hear about Greenland—not just because its melting ice would raise sea levels but because it's perfectly positioned to seriously muck up the ocean conveyer. If that conveyor ever stopped completely, we would see a significant turn of events. In fact, 14,000 years ago it probably did stop suddenly, triggering a mini ice age in Europe called the Younger Dryas.

ICE SHEET INSTABILITY

Glaciers are really slow-moving rivers of ice, flowing down to the sea. The faster they flow, the faster they dump ice, feeding into two feedback loops we've already talked about: the albedo effect and—in the case of Greenland—the ocean conveyer belt. Warmer temperatures make the glaciers flow faster, creating the feedback cycle.

But this particular phenomenon of melting glaciers has continued to surprise scientists, who keep discovering that it can happen much faster than we thought, with herky-jerky changes, as when the 12,000-year-old Larsen B ice shelf just sort of disappeared suddenly (over the course of a couple weeks) in 2002. There were a lot of jaws on the floor in the glaciologist community at the time.

This is why ice sheet instability is left out of the climate models—we know very little about how it works, except that it goes faster than we think it should.

FOR PEAT'S SAKE, ENOUGH ALREADY!

Warmer temperatures allow frozen peat bogs and other permafrost to melt, allowing the dead plant stuff to get on with the rotting it was doing before being frozen. Rotting peat releases both CO_2 and methane, driving the feedback loop.

Because the poles warm faster than the rest of the globe, all of the icy feedback cycles (methane gun, ice sheet instability, albedo effect, ocean conveyor, and permafrost) are pretty sensitive to warming.

Dissolve This!

Leave a glass of tap water out overnight, and in the morning there are bubbles on the sides. That's because as water warms up, less gas can be dissolved in it. The ocean is a huge carbon sink in part because CO_2 from the air dissolves in it. Heat that ocean up and less gas dissolves, meaning more CO_2 in the air, and the feedback continues.

Masks—but Not the Fun Kind

As if feedback loops weren't enough to make the warmers climb the walls, there's also the concept of "masking" effects— things that keep the warming *smaller* than it would otherwise be. That's a good thing in the short run because it gives us a little elbow room.

The concern is, if the masking gets "used up" or stops working, then the effects of global warming will accelerate faster than expected. A masking effect can be like a coiled spring—it takes up some of the shock now, but if too much pressure is put on it, it'll give a nasty backlash when it finally lets go. Scientists suspect that there are several maskings in the climate system.

GLOBAL DIMMING

Our industrial activities put out aerosols, which are tiny little particles in the air that reflect some of the sun's incoming energy. In terms of global warming, this is a good thing because by blocking some of the sun's rays, they keep us cooler. Kind of like atmospheric sunscreen. The ironic part is that as we clean up air pollution, we reduce that masking and therefore increase the warming.

Though aerosols have their downsides, like causing asthma and acid rain.

CARBON SINKS

Page 162.

Another masking effect comes from carbon sinks like the ocean and forests. Of the 10 Gt of carbon we emit every year, only about 5 Gt of it hangs around in the atmosphere long enough to have a greenhouse effect. That's because 2 Gt goes into the ocean as dissolved gas and in the bodies of little beasties. So the ocean acts as a sink, masking the warming that would otherwise be caused by those extra 2 Gt.

The ocean has a limited capacity for absorbing carbon, but we don't know what it is. It may one day sort of—well—stop absorbing, kind of like a saturated sponge. That would really suck because that would increase the amount of carbon emissions that would accumulate in the air every year from 5 Gt to 7 Gt, without us emitting even an ounce more. So suddenly we discover we need to cut our emissions even faster than we thought.

And where did that last 3 Gt go? It's a bit of a mystery. There must be a sink somewhere taking that stuff in—probably forests and such—but we haven't the foggiest idea of how resilient that sink is or how easily it could suddenly stop absorbing carbon, leaving our full 10 Gt a year in the atmosphere instead of our current 5 Gt.

If you really want to agitate warmers, point out to them that recent studies indicate that the carbon sinks are filling up even faster than the climate models had predicted. Watch 'em squirm!

All Together Now! Tipping Points

With all of those positive feedback loops feeding themselves, how is it that the climate is *ever* stable? There are negative feedback loops at play as well, such as increased clouds with higher temperatures, the weathering of rocks, and the most dominant one: the warmer that something (like the earth) gets, the faster it gives off heat. But the balance between negative and positive feedback loops in a complex system can be a delicate one, leading to another feature of such systems: *tipping points*.

These are points at which you no longer need to keep pushing for the change to keep going on its own, accelerating faster and faster with no further help. Sort of like slowly pushing a light switch: a small push consistently produces a small move, farther and farther until it suddenly flips all the way, leaving your finger hanging alone. Or that last half inch of scooching a microphone closer to its own speaker. Nothing, nothing, nothing, noth— ZWAAAAAAAAAAAAA!

Tipping points are scary because they can be hidden, sudden, huge, and irreversible (on a human time scale). Sometimes they're referred to as *points of no return*, which lead to *runaway effects*.

But, being an astute reader, at this point you're probably thinking, How dangerous can such tipping points be? All those feedback mechanisms have been at work in the climate forever, and humanity has adapted just fine. That's why there's such interest in studying the climate. We know it is a complex system, and we know complex systems can have hidden tipping points, so the big question is, Does the climate have any tipping points? and, if so, Where the heck are they so we can avoid them?

Unfortunately, there have been a couple of missing pieces of information in the pursuit of that question.

MISSING PIECE 1:
FEEDBACK IN THE CLIMATE MODELS

You know those computer climate models you've been hearing about? The IPCC report is based largely on them, and they are an easy target for skeptics, who point out that if we're no good at programming (or the data sets we put into them are flawed), then the results won't be any good. So why get worked up over something that's little more than conjecture? It sure seems that if you're a little off in your programming, then your results are likely to be a little off as well.

Except, with a complex system, a little off can end up turning into *way* off because of tipping points. When skiing along at the top of a slope, 6 inches to the left or right can make the difference between skirting the avalanche and ending up at the bottom of the mountain buried under snow. It depends on whether you hit that tipping point (which happens to be *that close* to a non–tipping point).

So here's the kicker that few people realize (including myself until a couple months ago), and it explains why some of the more flighty warmers are all in a tizzy: Most of the current climate models leave out several of the positive feedback loops described in this chapter (because they aren't well enough understood to model), which means there might be a tipping point right in front of us, and we don't know it. The models are better than nothing (remember, in a complex system you can still predict trends). But they aren't good enough yet to identify tipping points, which is the question of the day.

So to better answer the question of how the climate might behave in the future, a different chunk of climate researchers have looked in the opposite direction—the past. By studying things like ice cores and ocean sediments and the stoma on fossil leaves (no joke—these guys are übergeeks), they have put together a picture of how the climate has behaved over the last 3,000,000 years. And the picture they've uncovered hasn't comforted them.

This is the Big Secret that no one is talking about but that may change the whole ball game because it raises the stakes, shortens the timelines, and is based not on easily dismissed computer models but on knowledge of what the climate has actually done in the past.

By ridiculous amounts.

The NRC's 2002 report *Abrupt Climate Change* noted that this piece of the puzzle is a "new paradigm" that "has been well established by research over the last decade, but this new thinking is little known and scarcely appreciated in the wider community of natural and social scientists and policy-makers."

Page 110.

What they are talking about is our understanding of how long it takes the climate to change. As with all paradigm shifts, it took a while of being slapped in the face by the evidence before we accepted it. But the facts kept coming back, and eventually the data junkies bowed to empirical evidence.

Earth-scale processes take a long time compared to what we are used to. That's why the terms *geologic pace* and *glacially slow* are part of our vocabulary. Back in the early 20th century, we thought that the ice ages would come and go very slowly, with the transition creeping in over 50,000 years perhaps. As we got better at data collection and analysis, that number shrank, and the generally accepted wisdom changed as well. When we could resolve dates to within 10,000 years, and we saw a temperature difference of, say, 20°F between the beginning and the end of a 10,000-year time period, it was only natural to think "The climate gradually warmed by 20° over 10,000 years."

But a funny thing happened. When our methods got better so that we could resolve dates to within 1,000 years, we saw that the 20° change didn't happen smoothly over the whole 10,000 years. Instead, we found that it happened all

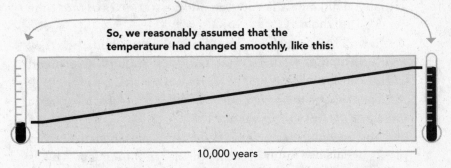

When all we could measure were 10,000-year chunks, we saw only the starting and ending temperatures.

So, we reasonably assumed that the temperature had changed smoothly, like this:

10,000 years

As our technology got better, we were able to measure smaller chunks of time, and we saw that the temperature change actually happened within just one of those chunks.

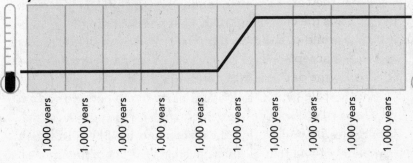

1,000 years 1,000 years 1,000 years 1,000 years 1,000 years 1,000 years 1,000 years 1,000 years 1,000 years 1,000 years

A new paradigm.

within a single 1,000-year period in the middle. Wow! That was surprising.

This was hard to accept at first, but scientists are slaves to data, so eventually the idea stuck, and our understanding changed.

As our methods got even better, and we could resolve time scales within 100 years, an absolutely mind-boggling thing happened. Remember that 20° change that we originally thought took 10,000 years, and then discovered that it really took place over the ridiculously short time of 1,000 years in the middle of that time span? You guessed it—we found that it had actually all taken place over the middle 100 years of *that* time period. Ulp.

Researchers continued improving their methods, and they now have good evidence that 14,000 years ago, Greenland warmed up by 20°F in just 50 years, with a change of up to 5° from one year to the next, and a reorganization of atmospheric circulation in just 1 to 3 years.

And recent research has discovered perfectly preserved plants uncovered by a retreating glacier in the Andes. "This is a soft-bodied plant," said glaciologist Lonnie Thompson. "It had to be captured by a very large snowfall at the time, a snowfall and climate change that began very abruptly; fast enough to capture a plant but not kill it. That is astounding."

So this is the new paradigm described by the NRC report and scarcely appreciated by the rest of us: Our climate has a hair trigger. One that can set off huge, sudden swings.

We now know that individual parts of the climate system may have their own tipping points (such as, the point at which it becomes inevitable that the Greenland Ice Sheet will melt completely), and that all those systems may combine into an overall tipping point for the climate, in which a few individual systems hitting their tipping points trigger the others, and off you go. This is the concept of abrupt climate change, and it appears to be the norm.

The New Picture: Two Dips and a Big Hill

Put together all of the information we've talked about in this chapter, and a new picture of our home planet's climate emerges. For the past 3,000,000 years, our planet has spent most of its time in one of two relatively stable states, glacial and the current interglacial, wobbling around in one of those little dips. A small push at the right time in the wobble—like a change in solar radiation (from orbital cycles or solar activity) or volcanic activity—provided the extra little "push" to get the climate over the hump and into the other dip.

It seems that in the past it has taken only small pushes to suddenly flip the climate into the other state. Flip, flip, flip. Back-and-forth through the ages. This is our history. Or at least the history of the earth. *Our* history—humanity's history—hasn't included one of these flips because civilization only came on the scene about 10,000 years ago at the start of the current interglacial period, and although global temperatures have fluctuated some since then, they've remained relatively stable.

What's got the nerdnicks all aflutter is the picture that emerges when we insert our current carbon transfer project into this new paradigm of how the climate normally behaves. Because science is quite sure that:

> Remind yourself of the time scales on page 154.

- CO_2 is a greenhouse gas,
- Greenhouse gases can possibly act as a *forcing*,
- Forcings can trigger tipping points, and
- Our climate has tipping points.

Put those together, and perhaps you can understand why some in the scientific community are all in a lather. As climate researcher Wally Broecker summed up: "Climate is an angry beast, and we are poking it with sticks." Even though the computer models haven't been able to give a definite answer yet about where the tipping points are, we do know that carbon levels in the air haven't been this high for millions of years. This is new territory,

> That's, um, not a pleasant metaphor. I prefer Mother Earth or the balance of nature. Something a little more benevolent.

and this is why the uncertainty of the models isn't a comforting thing to the warmers.

Warmers are concerned that our use of fossil fuels is pushing us farther and farther out of our stable little dip and up the slope of a neighboring hill. The peak of that hill might be a significant tipping point, a point of no return, beyond which the mutually reinforcing feedback mechanisms take off and we no longer need to keep pushing for the climate to continue rolling down the other side to undiscovered territory. So far, we've gone about 1.4°F up that hill, but due to the heat sink of the oceans, the amount already in the pipeline probably amounts to another 1.1°F we're committed to.

So the question of the millennium is, Exactly how high up is the peak of that hill? More to the point: What's the maximum level of carbon dioxide in the air that would keep us juuuust this side of that peak?

That is what the climate modelers are falling over themselves trying to figure out.

> The exact numbers are still quite debated, but the basic picture is not: We have experienced a certain amount of warming, there is a lag time in the system for temperatures to rise (so we have committed to a certain amount of future warming, even if we stop all emissions today), and we may be near a tipping point whose exact location is uncertain.

Firecrackers and Uncertainty

Let's say you've got a big firecracker strapped to the radiator hose of your car. You don't want to set it off, but you've got places to drive. So you do some research to figure out how long you can drive before it gets hot enough to blow up. You come up with an estimated time with a range of uncertainty (say, 20 minutes plus or minus 5) and head out for a place 14 minutes away. Should be safe.

After 12 minutes, your wife calls and says she just looked

> No, I don't know how it got there. Use your own imagination. I'm fresh out.

up the firecracker's serial number, and it's from a batch that is inconsistent in their ignition points. The updated range of uncertainty is plus or minus 10 minutes. Your estimate is still uncertain—in fact, it's more uncertain than it was before—but that uncertainty is not your friend. Sure, you might be able to get away with *more* than you'd thought (possibly up to 30 minutes). But you've also suddenly discovered you are currently in the danger zone. So do you keep driving? That's a choice based on your risk tolerance.

When we think about the uncertainty of scientific predictions, we have become accustomed to thinking about them in terms of overestimating the danger. But uncertainty cuts both ways. If the climate models are uncertain, then they may be underestimating the danger instead. Yet we are quite certain of what the climate is capable of from the study of its past. The great uncertainty is, What would it take to make it happen again? The only thing we can say *for sure* is that as long as we continue emitting, we keep getting closer to any tipping points that are out there.

Writing about the stunning discovery of Greenland's abrupt 20°F shift, one researcher Page 174. commented on how the pace of change predicted by the models compares to what actually happened 14,000 years ago: "Simulated climate shifts [produced by the climate models] are, however, considerably slower than the observed ones, lasting a hundred to a few hundred years." In other words, the skeptics are correct—the models don't do a terrific job of reproducing the real climate (in this case, what happened with the ancient climate). But that may not be much consolation to them because the models are apparently incorrect in the undesirable direction—producing changes that are *slower* than what really happened in the past.

The ironic part is that many of the skeptics have been calling the IPCC a bunch of alarmist Chicken Littles for a while now. But given the trends both in our understanding of ancient climate (that changes in the past have been more rapid than we thought) and in the modeling (that we've left out several positive feedback mechanisms), it may turn out that the IPCC's assessments are way too conservative. In fact, as I mentioned in Chapter 6, every time the IPCC issued a report with projections, the changes in the climate observed by the next report generally outpaced even the most pessimistic of the earlier projections.

Jiggling the Trigger: How Much Is Too Much?

We know an abrupt and catastrophic shift in climate is possible (in fact, that's how the climate normally works!), we know it can be triggered by a forcing (in fact, that's how the climate normally works!), and we know we're jiggling the trigger (okay, this part is new). So everyone's working like hell on the computers to figure out, Just how big of a jiggle might it take to set this thing off? While we continue jiggling the trigger. Perhaps you can see why the warmers are kind of twitchy.

Which brings us back to our bathtub. What has the warmers really alarmed is that even if we stop the rise of the water level in our tub and keep it at a steady level—a tremendous accomplishment itself in today's politics—hanging around at a higher level may carry with it a huge risk of triggering catastrophic consequences. Like, even if you halt the *rise* in your cholesterol levels, the longer you let them hang out at an elevated level, the more likely you are to have a sudden heart attack.

So the action warmers are now calling for is to move toward shutting off the spigot almost entirely and reaming out the drain. This would make for a net outflow of carbon from the atmosphere, at which point they would nervously wait for the carbon levels to creep back down out of the danger zone, which they hope would happen before the temperature triggers a tipping point.

This is what they're referring to when they speak of a "zero-carbon economy," and it's why you hear so much hubbub about renewable energies—sources like nuclear, wind, solar, and hydroelectric that do everything for us that the fossil fuels do but without emitting the carbon.

So what's a safe level of carbon in the atmosphere? The only thing everyone agrees on is that the estimates have been getting lower and lower as the science advances. As I mentioned earlier, business as usual would put us somewhere around 900 ppm by the end of the century. The warmers among the scientists used to say maybe 650 ppm would be a safe bet, and the policy makers said, "We'll look into it." Then the scientists said 550 ppm, and the policy makers said, "That's not feasible." Then the scientists lowered it to 450 ppm, and the policy makers said, "Are you out of your mind?" And now come James Hansen and company with their fancy-dancy peer-reviewed paper that says, "Actually only 350 ppm would be a safe bet."

The fact that we've already passed 350 ppm is not lost on Hansen, who is running around pointing it out to anyone who will listen. In fact, there's now a whole warmer movement started around that single number. It's called, well . . . 350.org.

Not so catchy, but you've got to give them points for clarity.

Doomsday Demystified Yet?

If you haven't noticed already, this book is largely about avoiding mistakes. You are being required by the world to place a bet on the global warming issue ("I choose not to bet" is choosing ticket B), and as you try to make the best decision you can, you of course want to avoid as many mistakes as possible. One

It's Not the Temp That Gets Ya: Demystifying the Doomsday

common mistake in life is to reject something because it is unreasonable, but then it turns out to be true.

This chapter has been focused on building enough of an understanding of where the warmers' doomsaying is coming from that you can see it's not unreasonable. The predictions may still end up being totally wrong, and we'll all have a good laugh about the mix-up a couple decades down the road. But they are not unreasonable, and so you would not be well served to dismiss them out of hand.

So now maybe you can better understand the warmers' point of view that the uncertainty in the science in general and the models in particular—far from being reassuring—mean that we may be in for some surprises. And that with a global, nonlinear system, there is probably no reset button. It appears to be a one-way ride.

This may not be right. But perhaps you see now that it isn't unreasonable.

CHAPTER 9

AUTHOR'S CONCLUSION: AS IF YOU COULDN'T ALREADY GUESS

At this point, you've acquired some powerful thinking tools, and you've seen a survey of the arguments in the shouting match. Now it's time to assemble a conclusion from all that. So here is the sample problem on the board where I illustrate how all the tools come together to bring some confidence out of uncertainty. The tools are intended to allow you to look at one of the most complex, high-stakes debates in history—filled with a haze of contradictory statements and a short timeline—and come out with your own, well-reasoned, tailor-fit answer to the question, What, if anything, should we do about global warming?

In the next chapter, when you'll use your own credibility spectrum and your own sources to make your own grid, I'll give you detailed instructions. Because you've already got the big picture of how this all goes together, for this chapter I'll just share my results, along with a new element I haven't talked about before: personal factors.

Page 101.

I make no claims of knowing The Truth. So you can assume that every sentence below starts with "It seems to me that . . ." although I've omitted those for readability.

Feel free to add them back in with your red pen if you start to feel like I'm getting preachy.

The Dressed Credibility Spectrum

While we were wading through the shouting match back in Chapters 6 and 7, I made note of why I would place each source at a particular level on my credibility spectrum. In the illustration on page 183, I've placed those sources on my spectrum, using acronyms or short names to save space. The exact placement of a source relative to the others around it isn't critical because I'm not so concerned with pitting any two statements head to head. My focus is on the big picture that emerges from dressing the spectrum.

When I first looked at my dressed credibility spectrum, the bottom half of it gave me a big *Aha* about why there seems to be such a disconnection between the high level of uncertainty in the public debate and the low level of uncertainty (as far as I can find) in the scientific literature. The media have an ingrained tendency to "tell both sides of the story," and there are a lot of very articulate sources on the skeptical side who are both ready to oblige and skilled in public relations (unlike the Nerd Patrol).

> At least, to a point. They don't go and get the views of the moon-hoaxer crowd when doing a story on space policy or interview Holocaust deniers when reporting on events in Israel.

The unfilled space at the bottom of the warmers' side isn't because of a lack of sources—there are, of course, many that could go there (think of how many scientists could be unpacked from the IPCC, AAAS, NAS, and joint national academies and listed individually)—but in looking for the most credible sources on both sides, I was able to fill up the entire warmers' chapter (Chapter 6) by the time I got down to adding individuals.

> Page 128.

If you recall, on the skeptics' side, I deliberately went looking for sources at the top of the spectrum in an effort to combat my confirmation bias but came up with only the noncommittal statement from AAPG. (Recall that EIA and AMG don't advocate a particular position; they are included here for their data.) That doesn't mean such sources don't exist, just that I didn't find them—though I feel like I made a sincere effort. (If you find some, please share them with me at www.gregcraven.org.)

> Page 147.
> Page 129.
> Page 147.

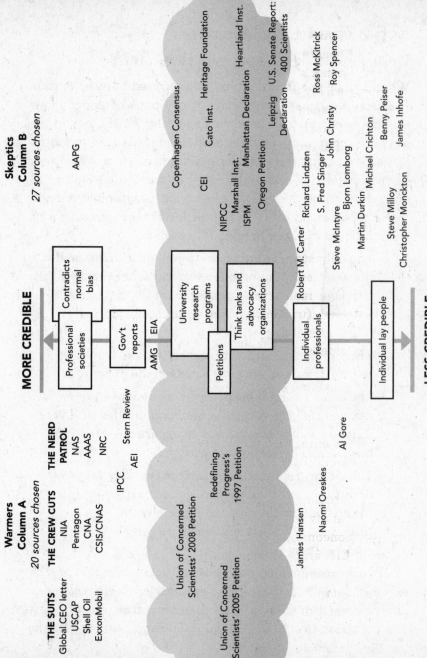

MORE CREDIBLE

Warmers
Column A
20 sources chosen

THE SUITS
Global CEO letter
USCAP
Shell Oil
ExxonMobil

THE CREW CUTS
NIA
Pentagon
CNA
CSIS/CNAS

THE NERD PATROL
NAS
AAAS
NRC

Professional societies

Contradicts normal bias

Gov't reports

AMG   EIA

IPCC

AEI

Stern Review

University research programs

Petitions

Think tanks and advocacy organizations

Redefining Progress's 1997 Petition

Union of Concerned Scientists' 2008 Petition

Union of Concerned Scientists' 2005 Petition

James Hansen

Naomi Oreskes

Individual professionals

Al Gore

Individual lay people

Robert M. Carter

Skeptics
Column B
27 sources chosen

AAPG

Copenhagen Consensus

CEI   Cato Inst.   Heritage Foundation

NIPCC   Marshall Inst.   Manhattan Declaration   Heartland Inst.

ISPM   Oregon Petition   Leipzig Declaration   U.S. Senate Report: 400 Scientists

Richard Lindzen   Ross McKitrick

S. Fred Singer   Roy Spencer

Steve McIntyre   John Christy

Bjorn Lomborg

Martin Durkin   Michael Crichton   Benny Peiser

Steve Milloy   James Inhofe

Christopher Monckton

LESS CREDIBLE

Finally, my credibility spectrum gets dressed.

183

Estimating Likelihoods:
Drawing the Rows of the Grid

When I sit back and look at my dressed credibility spectrum, I realize I don't need any fancy logic about whether to move the line on my grid up or down. Especially when I look at the top of the spectrum with its significant imbalance—and think about how strong the statements were from so many sources of such heft—it seems pretty clear to me: If that isn't good enough to move the line up, then what *would* good enough look like? So on my grid, I move the line between the rows way, way up, based on these factors:

- The **imbalance** at the top between the warmers and the skeptics. ("Consensus as strong as the one that has developed around this topic is rare in science," wrote Donald Kennedy, the editor of the journal *Science*, in 2001.)

- The significant **authority**, **expertise**, and **track record** of so many of the sources in the upper left.

- The fact that the same, strong conclusions were reached in three very different communities with very different interests and areas of expertise—scientific, business, and national security.

- The striking contrast between the typically reserved nature of many of the sources and the strength of the statements they made—especially the ones from the scientific and national security communities.

To *not* move the line way up would seem to be making the extraordinary claim that all those professionals from so many different fields in the upper left of my spectrum must be part of a conspiracy, or mind-bogglingly incompetent, or gullible,

GLOBAL WARMING	ACTION	
	A Significant Action Now	**B** Little to No Action Now
False		
True		

The bottom row is way more likely than the top.

or corrupt. That is, of course, possible. But I don't find it at all plausible.

I find the alternative explanation much more plausible: that those sources know what they're doing, but there are a few well-funded, well-organized entities that, for reasons of profit or ideology, seek to delay action. And the rest of us all have very human brains with glitches that play right into those calls for inaction. I wouldn't say we're dupes. I'd just say we're human.

For example, a strong distaste of government.

As often is said in science, extraordinary claims require extraordinary evidence. And I don't see anything resembling extraordinary evidence that the warnings from those professionals in the upper left of my spectrum are anything other than what they seem to be: very well-educated guesses about what is likely to happen, based on a tremendous amount of expertise and study.

Estimating Consequences: Filling in the Boxes of the Grid

For the same reasons I just mentioned for moving the horizontal line in the decision grid way up, I rely largely on the sources in the upper left of my spectrum to fill in the likely consequences in each of the boxes.

TOP LEFT BOX

None of those sources predicted anything approximating economic doom, and several very authoritative sources (Nobel laureate economists and global CEOs) predicted that being a leader in developing renewable energy technologies would be a net economic gain.

Indeed, T. Boone Pickens, a billionaire Texas oilman, is building the world's largest wind farm of electricity-generating wind turbines in his state. And he's not doing it to fight global warming or to Save the Environment. He's doing it because he sees profit, because Peak Oil "guaran- Page 153. tees" $300/barrel prices, because U.S. dependency on foreign oil compromises our national security, and because the massive flow of money to oil-producing nations makes the United States poorer: "There's no jobs created, no taxes paid and no profit made."

Converting to a renewable energy infrastructure has other advantages as well. The current fossil fuel infrastructure is highly centralized and, therefore, quite vulnerable to a terrorist attack or natural disaster. Renewable energy sources such as solar and wind can be much more spread out, making them more reliable and robust to a failure at a single point.

If it hasn't already arrived, Peak Oil is probably coming in the next decade, so re- Recall the Shell Oil CEO's prediction of a shortfall by 2015. newable energies are going to be developed fairly soon anyway, and the history of capitalism shows that the early innovators can make a ton of money.

Think Bell, Microsoft, Ford, GE, Goodyear.

And though my understanding of economics is limited, it seems that the U.S. government, in mobilizing to fight World War II, largely spent its way out of the Great Depression. So attacking climate change might actually be just the thing to address a recession. Shifting to a low-carbon economy, including building a massive new energy infrastructure, may be the greatest job-creation opportunity we've seen in a long time.

But before I ever started this grid business, I knew I was a warmer. If I want to end up fairly confident that my grid isn't significantly biased by my existing beliefs, in each box I should compensate *against* my bias. So instead of assuming the economic consequences would be positive (which is what would please my warmer bias), I'll assume consequences ranging from moderate cost to moderate gain. I can represent that with the midpoint: neutral face, no net economic consequences.

TOP RIGHT BOX

Overpopulation is a mathematical certainty that either *we* start to deal with in the next few decades or *nature* starts to do it for us. And as I mentioned, Peak Oil is also a certainty (or, as close as science can get to one) in our lifetimes. So that top right box, where we put a happy face in Chapter 1, is not going to be so carefree after all, even if the pocket-protector crowd is wrong about the threat of global climate destabilization.

Probably the most surprising talk you'll ever see on any topic is the one by Dr. Albert Bartlett on this subject.

Because my assessment of the top left was that the economic *costs* of action would probably be neutral, I would have to conclude that there would probably be no economic *gain* from avoiding that action in column B. So I could make an argument that neutral economic effects combined with certain Peak Oil and population issues should make for a frowny face in the top right box.

But this is the "win" box of the ticket, and my warmer bias doesn't want it to appear appealing, so my inclination would be to make it as negative as possible. Again, to compensate against my bias, instead of putting the most negative outcome I could argue for, I'll put the more positive neutral face.

BOTTOM LEFT BOX

I've often heard this objection: But what if human-caused global warming is true but we can't fix it or we screw things up in our attempts? Here, again, I'm going to go with the sources at the top of my credibility spectrum. I trust that they've thought of that.

Factoring in the same neutral economic consequences from the top left box, along with the energy independence and resistance to terrorist attacks that a decentralized energy infrastructure brings, an argument can be made for a smiley face. But, from the warmers' statements, I'm going to factor in the likelihood that we are already in for some negative consequences from climate change, making that box less happy. So to be conservative, I'll make it a neutral face instead of a smiley.

Again, this helps compensate against my bias, which would like to see a smiley face in this box so that ticket A looks more appealing.

BOTTOM RIGHT BOX

The statements from the sources on the top left of my spectrum paint an extremely dire picture for this box. The analysis of the national security sources carry particular weight with me because they contradict their normal bias (you don't expect the crew cuts to be all about preserving Mother Nature), and it is their profession to assess threats to the country. And rereading their statements . . . boy, the picture ain't pretty.

So that wad of extremely drastic predictions from such credible sources justifies a full-on grimace. I know that such a picture is just what my warmer bias would argue for, and so I should offset it a bit like I did for the other three boxes, but I just can't find a way to justify ignoring such a stunning agreement from all those different highly credible sources.

My Bet

Looking at my completed decision grid, with the huge difference in likelihoods and the huge difference in potential mistakes (top left vs. bottom right), I again realize I don't need any fancy calculation to decide which column is the better bet. To me, column A clearly offers a better chance of safeguarding our future.

It's important to note that although my conclusion turns out to be in almost exact agreement with the warmers on the

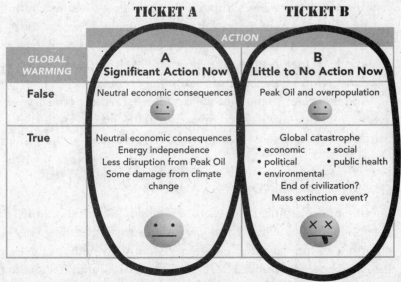

	TICKET A	TICKET B
	ACTION	
GLOBAL WARMING	**A** **Significant Action Now**	**B** **Little to No Action Now**
False	Neutral economic consequences	Peak Oil and overpopulation
True	Neutral economic consequences Energy independence Less disruption from Peak Oil Some damage from climate change	Global catastrophe • economic • social • political • public health • environmental End of civilization? Mass extinction event?

My completed decision grid.

top left of my credibility spectrum, my choice of columns is *not* because I am choosing to *believe* them. Remember, this whole risk-management approach was designed to get away from the need to choose who to believe. Rather, my risk assessment simply *uses* the *observation* that those statements were made to establish the probability of the rows.

But yes, sometimes when I realize how singularly focused I am on this issue, I start to wonder, Well, *am* I being too credulous? Then I remember, Oh yeah, it's not about believing them. I'm just using them to get a sense of what is most likely to happen in the physical world, what seems to be the best bet on which to place my family's security. And I find it highly unlikely that *all* those big brains on the top left of the spectrum are completely out to lunch. So I am very confident that the bottom row is much more likely than the top and that the bottom right mistake is much worse than the top left one.

Warning bells!!
Dunning-Kruger
effect? Page 69.

Does that make me a dupe? I don't think so. It's just how we get along in such a complicated, specialized world. But even if it turns out I am a dupe, at least I feel that I did my best to avoid it by making the most thorough, self-critical, conservative decision I can about protecting my family.

And it is clear to me that the best bet—the most conservative, careful bet—is to avoid any chance of ending up in that bottom right corner. So I'll take ticket A, please.

Personal Factors

Outside of the simple grid, there are personal factors that influence my conclusion. These are bits of my worldview—my experiences and values—that affect not only my choice of columns but how aggressive I think the action in column A should be. And how much of my butt I'll bust in pushing for that.

At this point I've made a big deal of identifying biases and guarding against them. But that doesn't mean that your background or experience or values or faith doesn't play a valid role in your decision. The key is to be deliberate about them. You don't want to be a slave to a grid. It is just a tool, an aid.

So, while the following factors are not part of the thinking tools I've laid out in this book, I think that they are a valid part of my decision about columns, as long as I'm being mindful of them. Your personal factors will of course be different from mine, but I share my own so that you can get an idea of how to go about incorporating yours in the next chapter. They will be especially useful to you if your grid ends up being less definitive than mine did.

As you read through the personal factors, keep in mind that you will be forming your own conclusion in the next chapter, so it might be useful to take some notes. You could jot down a simple "Yeah!" if you share a similar experience or value, or you might write a couple bullet points about how your experience is different from mine or how you think I apply my factors improperly.

MY RISK AVERSION

I am extremely risk averse when it comes to the welfare of my daughters. I much prefer risking the top left rather than the bottom right because even in the worst-case scenario of a great depression, I can still provide for my kids, while in the worst case of a catastrophically destabilized climate, there are unlikely (but feasible) scenarios that bring them serious harm. That, I'm not willing to risk.

I am also way more anal about bike helmets and seatbelts than most people I know, illustrating how one's level of risk aversion is a personal preference.

Because of this, I am not willing to wait until there is certainty on the issue (which there never will be anyway). I share the view of Thomas Schelling, a Nobel

Page 39.

Prize winner in economics: "This idea that costly actions are unwarranted if the dangers are uncertain is almost unique to climate. In other areas of policy, such as terrorism, nuclear proliferation, inflation, or vaccination, some 'insurance' principle seems to prevail: if there is a sufficient likelihood of sufficient damage we take some measured anticipatory action."

MY OBSESSIVE PERSONALITY

Unlike most of my other personal factors, my being obsessive argues against my choice of column A. I have a personal history of getting obsessed with an issue and blowing it out of proportion. And I hate to be wrong, so I can be a master of confirmation bias sometimes, looking to justify my beliefs. This can result in my having an entrenched view that some issue is tremendously important, when it later turns out not to be.

It is possible that a few years down the road, everything will be just fine, and I'll look back at myself now and just feel silly about how wound up I got. Given the statements and credibility of the sources in the upper left corner of my credibility spectrum, that doesn't seem likely. Still . . . here's hopin'. I just don't want to bet my kids' future on that possibility.

MY FAMILIARITY WITH COMPLEX SYSTEMS

Having studied complex systems some, I have a wary respect for how they can suddenly behave radically differently than expected. This would normally make me cautious, but knowing that several positive feedback mechanisms in the climate haven't been included in the current projections makes me downright jittery. This increases how aggressively I want to pursue column A.

MY HESITATION ABOUT OVERCONFIDENCE

As a science teacher, I am very aware that the history of modern science is littered with good ideas gone bad—cases in which we thought we understood things better than we did but ended up having unexpected consequences bite us in the butt later (like asbestos, PCB, thalidomide, the Castle Bravo nuclear test). So I prefer to err on the side of being more conservative rather than less. That way, if the unexpected happens, I've got some cushion rather than being immediately hurt.

The financial meltdown of 2008 provided a sort of practice run of what can happen when overconfidence is combined with a complex system like the climate (or the global financial system, in this case). Our faith in the ability of those in power to successfully manage a complex system was shattered over the course of "the week that broke Wall Street."

This is significant to the climate change debate because it highlights what I've been trying to suggest throughout the book: We are better served if we are willing to ask ourselves, What if this very confident statement I'm hearing from an expert turns out to be wrong? How much am I willing to bet that he's right? What's the worst that could happen if he's not?

One bombshell was the congressional testimony from former Federal Reserve Chairman Alan Greenspan, in which he admitted that he didn't know how the economy works as well as he thought he did. And well-known economic commentator Ben Stein explained that he didn't see the fall coming because "I assume[d] that the future will be much like the past, but sometimes it isn't."

> Sort of like my realization about assumptions with my retirement broker (page 50).

It's pertinent to note that mega-investor Warren Buffet's reputation came out improved, however, because he had been warning about just such a danger for years, even to the point that *Newsweek* magazine called him "alarmist" back in 2003. "He always thinks through what's the worst possible thing that could happen," said Buffet biographer Alice Schroeder in an interview.

The lesson I take away is that sometimes sounding the alarm and being an alarmist are two different things.

THE TREND I'VE PERCEIVED IN THE SCIENCE

Scientific thinking is all about finding patterns, and as a science teacher I can't help but notice this pattern. As I've watched the science get more confident over the last 20 years, the picture for this century has just gotten more extreme: the consequences more dire, the timelines ever shorter.

This doesn't mean we're doomed. The climate may always turn out be more resilient than we thought, and short-term variations might confuse our understanding of the trends (for instance, the recent acceleration of Greenland outlet glaciers may have just been due to a random fluctuation of warmer waters).

But if every time I turn the corner the picture just gets yuckier, I prefer not to place a large bet that the next corner will break that pattern and bring a happier scene.

MY EXPECTATION THAT THIS WILL TRUMP EVERY OTHER ISSUE

In studying how far-reaching the negative consequences of a couple degrees of warming can be, I have come to view every other concern or cause or care of mine—except for faith and family—as secondary to the issue of abrupt and catastrophic global climate destabilization.

That's because if the worst-case scenario comes to pass (it's not likely, but it seems increasingly feasible), I expect that all of the other concerns of mine either will be actively made worse by the climate catastrophe or will receive no attention from the body politic because we will be too busy dumping resources into a scramble for security. As the author Douglas Adams wrote: "[F]aced with so much that is absolutely critical, [one] can't afford the time for anything that is merely very, very urgent."

I mean, what's the likelihood I'm going to care about civil liberties when I'm just trying to find clean drinking water?

MY AVERSION TO FUTURE REGRETS

I hate having regrets. So part of my personal decision-making process is imagining regrets I might have in the future and then trying to avoid them. When I think of choosing column B and then losing, I expect I would be filled with regret, tragically wishing I had made a more conservative decision. Especially when I spent the world to buy just a couple more decades of business as usual.

When I think of choosing column A and losing, I feel okay. Because even if we pay a nasty price in the upper left box, I expect I will feel like I made the most thorough, careful, responsible decision I could with the information I had at the time.

I won't be happy. But I won't be filled with regret, either.

MY SHORT-TERM VS. LONG-TERM FOOT-SHOOTING HABIT

In my daily behavior, I tend to be very much an immediate-gratification kind of guy. I strive mightily to fight that because, intellectually, I realize I end up happier if I'm willing to sacrifice a little in the short run to improve the long run. Having shot myself in the foot so often due to my shortsightedness, I feel a significant aversion to the possibility of doing that with the climate by deferring action because it might hurt the economy.

I don't take economic risks lightly—I've been laid off because of a recession before, and it sucks. But it seems to me that since the economy is a human construction, it is therefore responsive to human solutions, whereas we have only minor control over the large-scale physical world. And even depressions end. Climate chaos may not.

This makes me much more tolerant of any economic risk in the upper left box of my decision grid because choosing column B seems susceptible to the foot-shooting mistake I so often make about choosing the short term over the long term.

MY SYSTEMS FILTER

Teaching physics and chemistry all day for years on end has seriously affected how I see things. As I view problems, I almost always look at them through the filter of, How is this thing connected to that thing? So when I think about how much humanity has expanded and prospered in the last couple hundred years, I can't help but see it as a series of interconnected systems, each necessary for our modern prosperity.

To me, it's like we've clawed our way out of the subsistence lifestyle by building an amazing truss out of all sorts of interrelated pieces.

During the credit crisis of 2008, it was as if one of the sup-

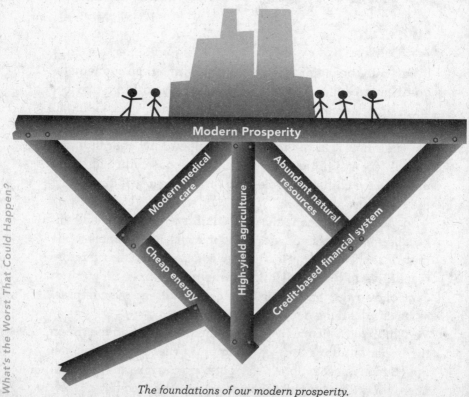

The foundations of our modern prosperity.

porting beams—our financial system—had abruptly buckled, and we all felt a stomach-wrenching lurch toward the abyss. It is extremely disconcerting to feel your foundation slip, and everyone suddenly became intensely focused on how to fix that failed beam before we all went pitching over the edge. The United States alone authorized more spending in just nine months of 2008 to shore up that beam than it did in all of World War II.

But when I zoom out, I see an even more fundamental beam that it is all built on—a stable, predictable climate.

As I described earlier, every bit of our modern civilization is based on the current climate. It Page 198. Page 154. seems to me that if that beam goes, so does everything else. So I take the financial crisis as a cautionary tale: Neglected maintenance of your underlying support structure can have extremely surprising and unpleasant consequences. This increases my motivation to choose column A, to ensure we don't experience an even bigger buckling.

I'M A SOFTIE

As a teacher, I'm a softie. Literally every day I am outraged by the circumstances that some one or other of my students is subjected to in his or her life. And so it is a powerful argument to me that global warming is simply unjust because it puts off the costs of our economic prosperity to the next generation. Our generation has earned its prosperity through hard work and innovation, to be sure, but it has all been based on our access to the cheap, easy energy that fossil fuels provide.

I believe that people who prefer column B love their kids just as much as I love mine. In my conversations with skeptics, it is clear that they are choosing column B because they think that it is more likely to safeguard their children's future. The reasoning I hear most often is that protecting the economy will allow us to be wealthy enough to deal with whatever happens.

Subsistence lifestyle

Current, stable climate

The wider view.

Modern Prosperity

Modern medical care

Cheap energy

High-yield agriculture

Abundant natural resources

Credit-based financial system

But living on credit—assuming I'll be able to find a way to pay the cost when the bill comes due in the future—doesn't necessarily work out. The analogy that we have lived it up at an expensive restaurant and are skipping out to leave the bill for our kids is a powerful image for me, and it affects how aggressively I want us to pursue column A.

I'M SELFISH

We know that humanity has adapted to climate shifts before. The species will go on. But to be honest, it's not the species I care about. It's me and mine. So assurances of, "We'll adapt" don't put my concerns to rest because it's the disruption and suffering involved in that process that I want to avoid. In all frankness, I'm so exhausted with all this that if it weren't for my kids, I might just sit back and watch the spectacle. But I can't. So here I am.

> What's that saying? The decision to have children is the decision to let your heart walk around outside your body for the rest of your life.

My Conclusion

When I look at all the stunningly strident statements from all those calm, professional sources in the top left, and I think, What are the chances they're all out to lunch? and then I add my observations that the predictions have only been getting more dire and more immediate as time goes on, it scares the willies out of me. So I vote for slamming on the brakes. Hard. I can recover from any hot coffee that I spill on my lap. But I can't put myself and my car back together if I drive confidently off a cliff, kids in the back.

Now What?

So, my tools have brought me to the conclusion that the safest, most conservative bet is to significantly reduce carbon emissions right away. What does that look like? And what do I do to turn my conclusion into action?

These issues stray from the purpose of this book, which is to equip you with the tools to make your own decision on the question of the millennium: What—if anything—should we do about global warming? The answer that my grid and personal factors lead me to is, Mitigate carbon emissions—aggressively. But this book has been about helping you decide for yourself what we should do. I don't want to go back on that promise by suddenly *telling* you what to do.

Still, it's not fair to leave you hanging. So how about a compromise? If after drawing your own conclusion in the next chapter it happens to agree with mine, I've included an appendix that lays out my personal vision for what can be done now that I've reached that conclusion. But I've set it off from the rest of the book to make it clear that it is optional and separate from the goal we set for ourselves in Chapters 0 and 1.

So no fair peaking at the appendix until you've done your final assignment. Now is the time you get a pencil, turn to the next chapter, and form your own conclusions about which is the best lottery ticket on which to wager your security.

CHAPTER 10

READER'S CONCLUSION: SOME ASSEMBLY REQUIRED

I've sincerely tried to give you some thinking tools in this book without slanting the text toward my own opinions on the issue. I'm sure they got through anyway.

> And I'm sure I'll hear all about it at www.gregcraven.org.

Like it or not, we are all forced by the laws of physics to make a choice between the two columns in our decision grid. Even if you think, "I don't need to choose. I'll just wait until the Labcoat Larrys finally get their act together and can prove what's going to happen. Last Geek Standing, that sort of thing," the laws of

> If you think only two columns is too restrictive, just keep reading. I'll meet you on the next page.

physics mark you down for column B because the climate waits for no one. It is right now running the experiment.

So now it's time for you to do your assignment.

Your task is to construct your own decision grid, and then use it to make your choice. You've already constructed your credibility spectrum based on your own values and experiences. Now it's time to use that spectrum to create your grid. You can do that however you want, and there is no correct method for doing so because, as far as I know, I made most of this stuff up—the credibility spectrum, using it to decide where to put the line in your grid, and the idea of looking at it as a choice of lottery tickets. So don't worry about doing it wrong. There has been no "right" established to check your choice against. There is only the eventual physical outcome (if any) of our actions on the climate.

There is going to be lots of simplification here. In fact, that's why you picked up this book—to help you simplify a complex issue so you can start to get a handle on it. Now, just like when you made your credibility spectrum, as you go about this exercise, don't worry too much about the specifics. Remember, this is supposed to be kind of fuzzy.

A couple small details going a little too far one way or another probably won't change the big picture. Your grid is not going to spit out The Answer; it is just going to give you a guideline for what to do. That guideline won't be perfect, and you will probably adjust it as time goes on and you get more information. But I'd say it's still better than the daze of confirmation bias most of us are left in without it.

There Aren't Enough Rows!
There Aren't Enough Boxes!
What Does *Action* Mean?

There are, of course, intermediate cases of action between the two columns. And intermediate possibilities for rows. And we haven't really detailed what *action* means—are we talking a fascist state in a New World Order or are we talking just encouraging people to buy A/C to ride out the summer heat waves? This can get as complicated as you like, which is why there are thousands of highly trained professionals slugging it out in literally tens of thousands of peer-reviewed articles.

You're welcome to go as far down the rabbit hole of unpacking the complexity as you wish, but don't fall for the trap of "letting perfect be the enemy of good." If you think the 2×2 grid is too oversimplified to be at all useful and you want to increase its resolution by adding columns and rows, that's fine. But, if you're like most of us, you won't end up following through on that, and so you'll be left with nothing instead of an oversimplified something.

I produced a version with 45 boxes in one of my videos, and each box contained 25 cases! Good times, good times . . .

Life is full of gray areas. And that's part of what this risk-management stuff is designed for—dealing with ambiguity. You can't know anything for certain, so let's get an approximate answer to reduce the chance that life is going to bite us on the butt. The only absolutes in this picture are the laws of physics (we think) and that what ends up happening is what ends up happening. The climate responds only to our choices, not to our beliefs, and so it's in our best interests to make some well-considered guesses rather than wait for the "right" answer. Because the only way to know what the right answer is for sure is in hindsight, after the experiment has run its course.

So I encourage you to just grit your teeth and do this exercise with the simple 2×2 grid to produce a provisional conclusion. Then later, if you wish, you can go back and make it more complex.

Step 0: Gather Your Biases

It might seem odd to stir up your biases when you're trying to avoid them, but that's part of the point. The most dangerous biases (and assumptions) are the ones you're not aware you're using. Better to have them in front of you, where you can keep your eye on them and check them against any decisions you're making—sort of like the antivirus program on your computer scanning for viruses by comparing copies of known viruses to what's coming in to see if there's a match.

Remember the Dunning-Kruger effect from page 69?

If you go looking for your biases and come back with, "I don't have any," then you should be extra careful. We've all got 'em. If you think you don't have any, that just means yours are still invisible.

Quick—spin around! Did you see any? Try again.

If you want, reread Chapter 3; it might be helpful.

> Or just ask your friends to identify your biases. I'm sure they would be happy to tell you what's wrong with you.

Step 1: Gather Your Statements

Assemble your statements and their sources. You're welcome to use mine or go find your own. Make note of any aspects of each source that would influence where you would place it on your credibility spectrum, such as its track record or authority.

Step 2: Transfer Your Personalized Spectrum

Recopy your credibility spectrum from page 99 onto the template on page 211.

Step 3: Hang the Ornaments

Dress your credibility spectrum like a Christmas tree, by placing each of your sources in its appropriate spot. There won't be room for the actual statements themselves, so use a name or acronym or an abbreviation to represent the source. Then when you look at your spectrum later, you can think, "Oh yeah, Copenhagen Consensus. That was the one with three Nobel laureates who did the prioritizing thing and put global warming at the bottom."

As you do this with one piece of evidence after another, over time you will start to see the big picture assemble.

And it will be unique to you—a personalized representation of how your values, experiences, and judgments filter the shouting match about global warming. How fun! But the really useful step is the next one.

> But, we hope, not biases, because you tried to guard against those in devising your spectrum.

Step 4: A Beautiful Christmas Tree

Now, here's the part that is both fun and potentially very difficult.

First, the difficult part. Try to consciously identify and then set aside not only your biases but what your current opinion on the debate is. Despite the tool of the credibility spectrum, this is still ripe ground for confirmation bias, because what you have in front of you is like that bucket of iron filings and black sand that I talked about earlier: a big pile of evidence that will make it really easy for you to come away feeling that your existing opinion is better supported by the evidence than is the contrary opinion. Try to keep in mind one of the fundamental aspects of science: letting the evidence form belief rather than belief select evidence. Ready?

Page 63.

Now, just like after you've finished decorating your Christmas tree, make a cup of coffee (eggnog, tea, cocoa, Red Bull, whatever), sit back, and just take in the whole thing at once. Look at the names of the sources and remember (or look up) what each one said. Maybe play out a little back-and-forth debate in your head between the sources to see if one side seems to have a really good point that the other side doesn't counter well. Add up Nobel laureates if that's important to you. Use this time to get a sense of how to make your grid.

> "I'll see your three Nobel laureates and raise you two."

There is no way to calculate this. What's important is that you play with it for a while, so that the spectrum itself gets a chance to make an overall impression on you.

Step 5: Decide Probabilities of the Rows

Based on the big picture of your dressed credibility spectrum, decide how likely the two rows of the grid are compared to each other. If you think they are equally likely, like a coin flip, draw the line separating the rows right in the middle of the grid on page 212. If you think the top row is more likely, represent that by drawing the line farther down, so that the boxes in the top row are bigger than those in the bottom. Draw the line far enough in one direction to make the relative sizes of the boxes generally represent the likelihood of the rows.

Step 6: Fill in the Boxes

Now fill in the boxes with future scenarios. I suggest first going back and skimming all the statements from your sources to look for what seem like the most likely consequences for each box. Then meditate on your dressed credibility spectrum for a bit to let the bits jostle around with each other for dominance. There will, of course, be many different possible scenarios in each box. You can either describe the range you think is most probable or just write down the middle scenario in that range with some question marks after it. I know it seems silly, but I do find the smiley/frowny faces useful for the last step.

Circle the first column and label it ticket A. Circle the second column and label it ticket B. Take a breather before the next step.

Step 7: Survey Other Factors

Like I did at the end of Chapter 9, spend some time thinking about other values or experiences that you would want to influence your decision. Write them down, so they're right in front of you as you mull over your decision. If you're having trouble coming up with any, it might help to go back and read through mine and note your reaction: You betcha! or You're crazy!

Step 8: Decide the Fate of the World

Just like you did with the credibility spectrum, play with the grid in your mind a bit, pitting the scenarios back and forth against each other. "Here I get cookies for sure, buuuuut over here I can get a whole cake if I'm willing to risk the killer bunny." Again, there is no way to know what the right answer is.

But there is a way to make sure you get a *good-quality* answer. And that is to have firmly in your mind the reasons you chose one ticket over another. Be able to say it in a sentence. I've found that if I can't, then my thoughts are not clear enough, which might indicate my confirmation bias—that I haven't let myself see something. Making a list of bullet points can help. Publish them on the web.

> Or come to www.greqcraven.org and share your grid with others. There are flame wars and overconfident pronouncements aplenty on the wild wild web but, as far as I know, no debates in which both sides share some common tools to try to get closer to agreement.

Install This into Your Brain

In the future, as you get a new piece of information or insight, resist the temptation to change the grid based on that one bit of information. It is important to not monkey with the grid directly, because that would bypass two very important safeguards:

- **Not giving one source too much weight.** New information should be added onto the credibility spectrum so that it can contribute to the big picture. Then, if that big picture has changed substantially, update your grid based on your *updated spectrum*—not on a single new piece of information.

- **The little red flags you've installed in your head.** They are the key to guarding against your brain's all-too-human pitfalls: confirmation bias, the tendency to deny big problems it'd rather not think about or believe, and the mismatch between the nature of climate change and your brain's innate alarm system.

These safeguards are the key to us getting anywhere in the discussion of what—if anything—should be done about climate change. One of the main points of this book is that it does not serve your interest to bypass them.

> As described by Daniel Gilbert on page 72.

Now What?

If your choice is column B, then congratulations! You've got a head start. Because business as usual (inaction on climate change) is where we've been sitting for a long time; it is the default. That does give the column B-ers a bit of an unfair advantage in the whole public policy debate. But what are you gonna do?

For you column B-ers, I've provided some links that may be useful to you in the "Further Resources" section in the back.

If your choice is column A and you're at a loss as to what to do about that, then I've got some suggestions for you in the appendix and in "Further Resources" in the back if you wish to get involved. But really, who am I to say how to influence a national debate? I've never done this before. If you have some good ideas, come to www.gregcraven.org and share them with others.

Either way, I hope you have been able to use the tools in this book to arrive at a conclusion that feels more rational, more thoughtful, more informed, and more likely to bring you a favorable result than before. And as a bonus feature, I'm hoping that this book will allow people on both sides of the debate to start listening to each other and working together to get closer to a common understanding, rather than continuing to shout past each other.

Because you've got to admit, no one likes the shouting, and it doesn't seem to have moved us very far forward in the debate. So perhaps we can do this in a different way, by all using some common tools in the discussion. There's always hope.

And that you have taken the time and energy to think through the issue certainly adds to *my* hope. Thank you for that.

**Warmers
Column A**

MORE CREDIBLE

**Skeptics
Column B**

↑
│
│
│
│
│
│
│
│
│
│
│
↓

LESS CREDIBLE

Your personalized credibility spectrum.

GLOBAL WARMING	ACTION	
	A **Significant Action Now**	**B** **Little to No Action Now**
False		
True		

Your personalized decision grid.

Now What? How _You_ Can Change the World

You're reading this appendix because your conclusion matches mine, and you agree that we should swing into action to mitigate climate change by significantly reducing carbon emissions. So how do we make that happen?

> Although I speak much less equivocally here for the sake of readability, as always there is a silent "It seems to me" in front of every sentence. Who am I to say what The Truth is?

I'm no climate scientist, and I'm no policy analyst. I would make a mess of both. So I'm not going to discuss policy options here. But you and I _are_ the executives in the picture: in charge of taking the scientists' bottom-line assessment of the issue, deciding what level of resources to devote to the problem, and then delegating to the policy makers the task of coming up with the best solutions.

What we do is give the word _go_.

It Is Much Later Than We Thought

Page 125.

As I detailed earlier, James Hansen has the best track record for making predictions about how the climate works and then having the mainstream scientific view eventually catch up and vindicate his assessments. So I propose we adopt his targets for what we should achieve. That doesn't mean he's right, but when betting on a horse race, you take a look at the track records of the horses. I can't find a more accomplished horse in this race, so I'm going to place my bet on him.

Plus his target—an atmospheric carbon concentration of 350 ppm—is the most ambitious out there, because his goal is the most conservative: to leave some room for error in ensuring we don't doom our modern prosperity. And I'm all over that goal.

Yet the implications of adopting his target are almost staggering, because in 2009 we are at 388 ppm (and accelerating away), and every passing year brings a greater likelihood of coming to a tipping point. It's a lot like having a high cholesterol level: It doesn't so much make you sick as it means that you have an increased chance of a heart attack. Which would make you suddenly very sick. Remember that he called the current European Union target of 450 ppm "a guaranteed disaster," which would eventually melt all the ice at both poles, raising sea levels by 75 meters!

If you recall from the bathtub discussion, we are currently not only opening the spigot farther but are spinning it open faster and faster. If we need to get the water Page 162. level back down to 350 ppm, there are a lot of steps between here and there: We need to slow the spinning, then stop the spinning entirely, then crank the handle almost shut, then ream out the drain, and then wait in suspense as the water level in the tub creeps down over time—and hope that we don't pass a tipping point before we get to the 350 ppm safe haven. The more time we are above that line, the greater the risk we run of triggering abrupt and catastrophic climate destabilization, which isn't a fun-sounding thing.

So we need to act with the greatest of urgency. Because of the lag times at each step of the way—changing policy, building a new energy infrastructure, waiting for carbon levels to drop, and then waiting for the climate to respond—it is like steering a huge ship whose massive inertia means it takes forever to turn. If you want to avoid an obstacle, you have to be watching the horizon and start the turn way ahead.

If you wait until the threat is obvious, it'll be too late to turn fast enough to miss the obstacle. At some point, the collision becomes inevitable, no matter what else you do.

In my book, the most intense 2 minutes in cinema comes from the 1997 movie Titanic. It kills me to watch them with the engines full astern and the wheel hard to starboard—they've done everything they can, and the ship just keeps crawling straight toward the iceberg. Argh!

Our energy economy—our fossil fuel infrastructure of drill rigs, coal mines, pipelines, railcars, diesel-burning trucks, gas-burning cars, coal-burning electric power plants—is that huge ship. It is this ship of our energy economy that we are steering, full steam ahead, straight at an iceberg.

So perhaps you can understand why I'm not going to talk about taking personal action in terms of changing your lightbulbs or turning down the thermostat and wearing a sweater. Doing those will definitely save you money. But what is required at this point is nothing less than a breathtaking

So say our lookouts—the scientists—trying desperately to get us on the phone.

change in the way the world produces and consumes energy, and Ten Convenient Ways to Reduce Your Carbon Footprint is great, but it isn't going to get us there.

Now that you understand the momentum of the climate system, the magnitude of our carbon transfer project, and the sudden nature of complex systems, you probably realize that at this point, the game is different.

It is much later than we thought.

How Soon?

What do you do when what is necessary is not politically feasible?

The timeline Hansen and his colleagues call for, while perhaps a good bet in terms of how the climate works, sure seems like a political long shot; based on his understanding of the science, Hansen says if we want to avoid triggering a tipping point in this jumpy climate system, we need to completely halt emissions from coal by 2030, including an immediate moratorium (supported by the USCAP) on building new coal-fired plants. That means we need to be on a very different track by 2015. And that means we must fundamentally change policies within, um, the next couple years. Sorry.

Which provides 50 percent of the electricity in the United States.

Page 115.

It's because of those darn lag times! Other peer-reviewed papers echo Hansen's message, detailing how draconian the actions may need to be if we wait even just a decade. They could always be wrong. (Let's hope so!) But how much do you want to bet on that possibility? It sure seems we are wagering the world, so I say let's go for Hansen's timeline.

But it sounds impossible, doesn't it? There's simply no way that social and political change can happen fast enough to fundamentally reorient our energy policies in just a year or so. I thought so, too. But then I realized that my conclusion—that 1 or 2 years is too short for significant social and political change—rests on an assumption I didn't know I was making.

Like Douglas Adams said on page 13.

My assumption was that political change would happen in the future in the same way it has in the past: slow, grueling, contentious, and messy. But that assumption isn't necessarily true. We have done the seemingly impossible on a ridiculously short timeline in the past when we put our mind to it. In World War II, the United States went from a standing start to the world's strongest, most productive economy in just 4 years, demonstrating that what is practical, or even possible, depends entirely on the context.

Your idea of what you can accomplish changes in an emergency.

World War III?

When Pearl Harbor was bombed on December 7, 1941, the United States undertook perhaps the greatest economic mobilization in the history of the world. Breathtaking production goals were set and exceeded. In the War Bond drives, the government asked citizens to "dig until it hurts, and then dig some more," and the people responded, investing an average of 25 percent of household income so that the goals were exceeded every time—sometimes almost doubled.

The U.S. war effort on the home front showed that massive government action, when driven by the people, can accomplish the seemingly impossible in an amazingly short amount of time. And it can do so without dooming the economy. In fact, the collected effort of the citizenry, pointed in a common direction, brought the United States out of the Great Depression and produced the world's strongest economy.

We need such a war-scale mobilization now, to once again ensure our security and to safeguard our very way of life from an imminent threat. We always thought that World War III would be an all-out nuclear exchange between the superpowers, and would result in the destruction of civilization if it were ever fought. But perhaps WWIII will instead be the War on Warming and, in an ironic twist, will result in the destruction of civilization if it is *not* fought.

The magnitude of the task laid out before us is so great that it is easy to despair, to think there is no way we can do so much so fast. But I have no doubt that if tomorrow everyone woke up with the thought "After my faith and my family, this is the most important thing to me"—if our reflexive response to requests became, How can I help? instead of, What's it going to cost me?—then we could do this easily, with a minimum of disruption.

Imagine what could be accomplished if we harnessed the

will, resolve, and ingenuity of all people moving in the same direction, striving together in a shared endeavor.

Rousing the Giant Within

Technologically, we can radically reduce carbon emissions quite handily. New breakthrough technologies can make it easier, but we've already got, right now, everything we need to accomplish the task of transforming our energy economy away from fossil fuels. Except the willingness.

The biggest obstacle here is that our adversary—which could spur us to make the effort—doesn't have a face. The Russians spurred the moon effort. Hirohito and Hitler spurred mobilization for World War II. But the enemy that's now threatening our very civilization is an invisible, odorless gas that comes out of our tailpipes. Whoa! Batten down the hatches! Plant a victory garden! Buy War Bonds! Doesn't really stir the soul, you know?

And there lies the biggest obstacle.

That's why climate law expert Mary Wood says we would be better off if we were attacked by aliens, and why Harvard psychologist Daniel Gilbert claims that if global warming had been visited upon us by a brutal dictator, the War on Warming would be this country's highest priority.

As described by Gilbert on page 72.

Climate change plays right to the *weak* spot of our brains' alarm systems: It is impersonal, amoral, and seemingly distant and gradual. Rather than being a strength in the challenge, our intrinsic human nature—an alarm system tuned to tangible threats—may be our undoing.

We can accomplish simply tremendous things when we set our collective mind to it. The looming threat now is, Will we set our mind to it in time? Will we rouse the sleeping giant ourselves, before it is roused—too late—by obvious disaster?

Though we now think that these last two aren't true after all.

A Word Against Optimism: Toward a New Ethic

While I was working frantically on this book, a neighbor sent me an email with the subject line "Inspiration for your book." It was this quote from Dee Hock, founder of Visa: "It is far too late and things are far too bad for pessimism." I suppose my neighbor meant it to help my mental state, to calm me down so I wouldn't go striding around with a frown on my face quite so much. But it turned out to have quite the opposite effect on me: I felt uncomfortable. Then scared. Then confused and agitated as to why I felt uncomfortable and scared. It was like an everlasting gobstopper of negative feelings. It took me a while to put my finger on it, but I eventually figured out why it disturbed me so.

Optimism is always considered a positive trait. But it can be tremendously harmful because it checks the urge to go all out. It hamstrings you. By feeling that things will work out, you are demotivated because, well, things will work out.

But pessimism does the same thing. By thinking that there's no way it will work out, you are also demotivated. Why work for something when the outcome is already determined? Both optimism and pessimism seem to be a sort of throwing up of the hands, a surrendering to the whims of fate. And that is absolutely *not* what we need right now. We need to realize that whether things work out okay or not depends on the choices and effort we put in right now.

When I'm thinking about these things, the image that invariably pops into my mind is from the World War II poster of Rosie the Riveter, the individual citizen rolling up her sleeves to answer the call of duty, to do whatever is necessary to preserve the world she loves. It is the embodiment of the mind-set we need at this moment.

We don't have a name for that attitude. It's neither optimism nor pessimism. I think we should be able to refer to it easily, but I can't come up with any name other than ... Rosie-ism. As in "I'm a Rosieist."

I know it doesn't roll off the tongue. But every time I get disheartened and feel like just giving up, I think of that poster, of her staring at me and rolling up her sleeves, and I rouse myself to continue plugging away. How can I just roll over in despair while Rosie is out there working her ass off?

Personal Actions: Trigger a Declaration of War

So how do we—you right there, and me right here—get this declaration of WWIII started? What concrete actions can *you* take tomorrow that will increase our chance of ending up in column A?

To turn the ship of our energy economy quickly enough, we need huge policy changes, and policy makers respond to

ISSUE	THE PESSIMIST SAYS . . .	THE OPTIMIST SAYS . . .	ROSIE THE RIVETER SAYS . . .
The classic "Hey, look at this glass of water!" test.	The glass is half empty.	The glass is half full.	Enough philosophizing. Let's find some more damn water.
Can we do it?	Give up. It'll never get done.	Relax. It'll get done.	Let's get to doing it.
Faced with an overwhelming situation.	We're doomed!	Everything's going to be fine.	Work like hell!
What are the odds of succeeding?	It's impossible.	Where there's a will, there's a way.	Not available for comment.

Optimism, pessimism, and Rosieism.

Out working!

only two things: hordes of constituents and lobbyists. Lobbyists are employed by businesses, which respond to hordes of consumers. So basically, the hordes have the ultimate power. Point the hordes in the right direction, and we can accomplish most anything.

What can you personally do to rouse the hordes? Here, I think we can take a lesson from the climate. One of the things that makes climate change so frightening is that it is a complex system, capable of huge changes being triggered by tiny events. Well, in today's wired world, our society is also a complex system, with lots of interconnections and feedback loops. Which means it is capable of huge changes being triggered by tiny events.

While this is sometimes called the butterfly effect (the idea that the flapping of a butterfly's wings in Asia can set off a hurricane in the Gulf Coast), a more concrete example is that of Rosa Parks: an ordinary woman who was in the right place at the right time and set off the civil rights movement with her simple action of refusing to move to the back of the bus. A few pebbles kicked downslope in the right place can set off an avalanche.

Today, with email, cell phones, personal organizers, text messaging, BlackBerrys, Facebook, YouTube, MySpace, Twitter, blogs, and god knows what else, there is at this very moment an interconnected web of communication that permeates our society. *That* is the avalanche poised on the slope—an explosive spread of awareness and will, just waiting to be triggered.

Go Viral, Baby!

What do you do to trigger it? The answer is deceptively simple: You spread the word.

Your most immediate goal is not to change your lightbulbs or write your representative, but to spread the awareness of the situation far enough and fast enough so that a policy maker can't turn around without having a clump of constituents in his or her face demanding, "What are we going to do about climate change?" You harness the nonlinear nature of our communications culture to kick some pebbles down the slope, trying to set off the avalanche. It is possible for a single ordinary person, in the right place at the right time, to have a huge effect.

If that sounds like the spread of a virus, that's because it is. The scientist Richard Dawkins coined the term *meme* to mean an idea that spreads like a virus, and the author Malcolm Gladwell coined the term *social epidemic* to describe the spread itself. That is exactly what I'm talking about: a viral spread of the meme that we should change the question in the global warming debate from, Is it true? to, Why risk it?

Man, I could learn a thing or two about coining catchy terms from these guys.

To really get a sense of how powerful this strategy is, it's useful to understand the nature of an actual virus. A virus has no resources of its own. All it has is instructions—a blueprint on how to make another copy of itself. So how can a single measly packet of instructions cause an epidemic? Because it infects a host and enlists the host's resources, experience, and contacts to make many copies of itself, which then spreads to other hosts. The original virus doesn't need resources, just information, because it hijacks the resources of its hosts along the way.

And here's the key part:

When those copies go on to infect other hosts, each new copy of the virus is carrying the same pass-it-on instructions that the original did.

So if the instructions say, "Make 10 copies and spread," each of those 10 copies carries the same instructions, so the next round sees 100 new copies, and the next round 1,000, and on and on. It's absolutely crazy growth. In fact, it's exponential, which is nonlinear, which is like the climate itself. In that sense, we can fight fire with fire.

So that's how we can change the culture: you take it upon yourself to get 10 people interested in using the decision grid (or asking, Why risk it? or looking at credibility, or the seatbelt principle, or however you package it), and you tell each of them to *pass it on* to 10 more people with the same instructions, and so on. In just five steps, that's over 100,000 people who have thought about global warming in a new way. Because of *you*.

No one can know for sure which are the exact pebbles that will trigger the avalanche. But what you do know for sure is that the more kicking that happens, the more likely the avalanche is.

Could you be the one in the right place at the right time with the right idea? Could you be someone who stands next to the trigger of history, unaware of your own significance in the whole picture, but whose single action might change the course of the world? Could *you* be the pebble kicker who sets off the avalanche?

Probably not.

But . . . quite possibly so. The only way to know is to go ahead and kick those pebbles down the slope. I know how busy most of us are, so it's easy to think, Why bother? if the chance of your action having significant consequences is so small. But think back to the nature of nonlinear systems: You never know when a tipping point might be reached, so that a small action ends up triggering huge changes.

Instead of your small action being just a drop in the bucket (with just a small result), each action might instead be that last

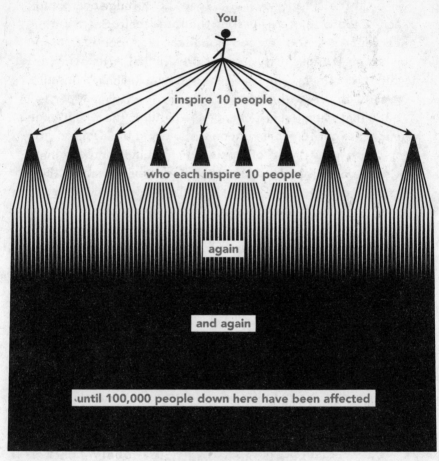

BECAUSE OF YOU.

The power of one: kicking pebbles down the slope.

scooch forward, pushing the system over the edge of a tipping point, setting off an explosive feedback cycle. Small action, huge result.

So, rather than "a drop in the bucket" or "every little bit helps," a more accurate analogy is to picture each small action you take as a lottery ticket. Like a lottery ticket, your action has only a very small chance of paying off. But the prize is the world. Even if you don't buy a winner, it is at least a satisfying undertaking because it eliminates the sense of powerlessness in the face of an overwhelming challenge. And the more tickets you buy, the greater your chances.

That's why it's fun to play: Each ticket holds the promise of the jackpot. And unlike the lottery, the tickets are free.

Want one?

BE *THE VIRUS*

So you've been infected with the idea and you want to buy some save-the-world lottery tickets by spreading the word. What you do now is think of yourself as the host of the virus and get it to mutate and spread. You brainstorm: What resources do I have? What talents do I have? What contacts do I have? How can I spread this viral idea, this meme?

> Ewww . . . are you sure this is a good analogy?

Remember, you're *not* spreading the message of OhMy GodWe'veGotToDoSomethingAboutGlobalWarming!! because that message has worked some, but only at the normal pace of social change. Instead, you are spreading the meme of asking people to think rather than telling them what to think. Of changing the question from, Is it true? to, What's the worst that could happen?

Always keep in mind that the key part to making the growth exponential is that your message contains the instructions "Pass it on." Otherwise you are just campaigning, which is the old way that cultural change happens. And we simply do not have time to wait for that to happen. If we want to save our bacon, we need exponential growth in political will—we've got to transform *how* social change happens by harnessing the nonlinear, the viral.

We change the culture by finding the memes that spread *themselves* through the whole society, through every demographic, from redneck to hippy, beer-chugger to latte-sipper, Wall Street to Main Street. We cannot afford for this to be another campaign. We are in a time like no other, a problem that can be solved only by a change like no other: a social epidemic, enlisting people and resources as it goes.

Things to Do

How might you go about this?

I suppose I shouldn't miss this opportunity to suggest that you devote some of every paycheck to buying multiple copies of this book and handing it out like candy.

No joke—one guy told me he plans on leaving copies in random places where it will be picked up, like Laundromats and stuff. How eerie would it be if you're reading these words right now . . . and you picked this up in a Laundromat!

There are, of course, other less lucrative-to-me ways to spread the meme. The wonderful thing here is you can pick a level of action that matches the amount of time and energy you feel you can give. Each action, no matter how small, is a lottery ticket that may be the one to pay off. If you want greater chances, get more tickets. If you don't have any time, get just a couple. Give yourself permission to scale your actions to your life. It provides a magical flexibility that is empowering. And more gets done that way, because you don't let perfect be the enemy of good.

The easiest way to spread the meme is of course to simply

forward the videos this book is based on to family and friends. A few clicks and you're done.

A little more active method is to incorporate the ideas from the book into your thinking and your conversations. You don't have to be an annoying crusader to make a difference. Just something along the lines of responding to, "How was your weekend?" with, "You know, I

Links at www .greqcraven.orq, or just Google around and you'll find them, perhaps along with interesting things that other people are doing. Hey—interconnections! Feedback! Tipping points!

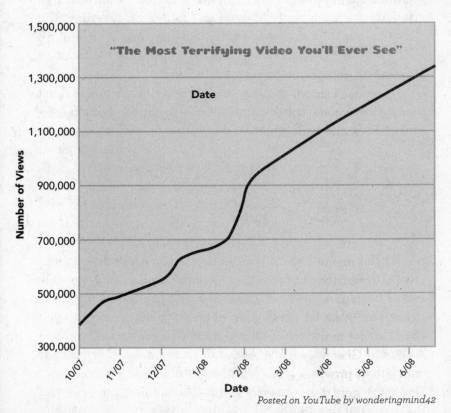

"The Most Terrifying Video You'll Ever See"

Date

Number of Views

1,500,000
1,300,000
1,100,000
900,000
700,000
500,000
300,000

10/07 11/07 12/07 1/08 2/08 3/08 4/08 5/08 6/08

Date

Posted on YouTube by wonderingmind42

Find the multipliers.

came across this interesting grid argument that got me to thinking . . ." As you go about this, keep in mind that people tend to respond better to questions than demands. So instead of saying, "Listen to this!" start off with, "Hey, what do you think about this?" And then be sincere in listening to their answers.

Here's a key point I discovered with my videos. Take a look at the graph on the previous page of the number of views for my "Most Terrifying Video You'll Ever See."

You see that vertical part? Just what the heck happened in mid-January? What happened is that the video got featured on Yahoo!'s homepage. So for about 24 hours, everyone who went to check their Yahoo! email account saw a little blurb about the video, and as a result over 100,000 of them watched it in one day!

Here's the wild thing to think about. That action—putting that blurb on the homepage—was probably a decision by a single person on the Yahoo! team. That person is an example of what I call a *multiplier*—someone whose position or connections or personality makes him or her a hub. Get the right person on board, and you get more accomplished than months of exhausting effort on your part.

So lobby multipliers: journalists, authors, pundits, columnists, celebrities, executives, elected officials, bloggers, talk show hosts (TV and radio), charities, nonprofits, advocacy organizations, think tanks, lawmakers, musicians, experts you see quoted in articles, political candidates, producers, directors, athletes. Repost the videos on other video sharing sites or click on the Digg It or Reddit or Stumble Upon button, enter it into contests, or borrow the arguments and make your own videos with your own spin and enter those into contests. Brainstorm with friends on how to do some guerilla marketing no one's ever thought of before. Make little business cards with the decision grid on one side and the words *Pass It On* on the other and just sort of leave them around wherever you go. There are already a number of discussion forums online that sprang up from my videos—find some of those and trade ideas. Coordinate a flash mob. Hire a skywriter. Saturate! We don't necessarily need a genius. We just need a million people trying a million different things.

Here's a key term that you can use to find other people interested in these ideas: Manpollo (as in the Manhattan Project and the Apollo Project combined). It's a holdover from my videos, but it has the advantage of being unique to my ideas because I made it up.

Focus on burning the number 350 into the collective consciousness. It is an easy meme: concrete, short, independent of language, and emblematic of a threshold that may possibly mean the difference between the preservation of our civilization and the final fall. Hook up with www.350.org—the site has pictures of people doing amazing and wacky things to call attention to that number—or just start writing *350* everywhere you go.

That's not exaggeration—recall Ward's hypothesis from page 151.

Given the trends in the predictions of climate science (always worse, always sooner), I suspect that 350 will go down in history as "humanity's number"—a symbol of our collective fight for our civilization and an emblem of the challenge that finally united humanity to struggle together, instead of against one another.

You may be inclined to reduce your carbon footprint significantly or do some direct action. (I've heard calls from some scientists that people should be chaining themselves to coal plant smokestacks! Ouch!) But if you really want to go big, the greatest bang for your buck is to focus on spreading the idea of risk management in an exponential fashion by always including the idea of passing it on in your message.

Take the energy you would normally put into going green and pour it all into spreading the word, to trigger a wholesale change in the culture within 2 years. This can't just be another grassroots campaign for some worthy cause, because we simply don't have time for that. The exponential curve of global warming can be caught only with another exponential curve.

We Can Do It

So much of what is required of us echoes the challenge the United States faced in mobilizing at the start of World War II. It seems overwhelming, as if there's no way we can possibly muster the will to act in sufficient time and scale. But that generation did it. Perhaps we can too. So if your hope or your energy starts to fade, think of Rosie, and revisit President Roosevelt's words at the onset of the war, when he faced the daunting task ahead with grim determination:

> *Difficult choices may have to be made in the months to come. We do not shrink from such decisions. We and those united with us will make those decisions with courage and determination. . . . Our task is hard—our task is unprecedented—and the time is short. . . . We know that we may have to pay a heavy price for freedom. We will pay this price with a will. Whatever the price, it is a thousand times worth it.*
>
> *We are fighting today for security, for progress, and for peace, not only for ourselves but for all men, not only for one generation but for all generations. . . . That is the conflict that day and night now pervades our lives.*

So can we do it? Based on the spirit and sacrifice displayed by Americans during the economic mobilization for World

War II and on the nonlinear nature of modern communications, I believe we can.

Will we do it? Will we rise to the greatest challenge in human history—to be wiser, better than we have ever been—to choose to act rather than be forced to act? Well that, in part, depends on what you do next.

Tag. You're it.

FURTHER RESOURCES

THE BASICS OF GLOBAL CLIMATE CHANGE
These sources are quite objective and credible:
- www.aip.org/history/climate/links.htm
- http://green.nationalgeographic.com/environment/global-warming/gw-overview.html
- www.pewclimate.org

SKEPTIC SITES
These are useful sites with skeptical resources not already mentioned in the text:
- www.co2science.org (A well-established and continuously updated clearinghouse of information)
- www.climatescience.org.nz (A number of heavyweight figures are involved with the New Zealand Climate Science Center, including Bob Carter, Vincent Gray, and David Bellamy—all scientists, though none in climatology)
- www.worldclimatereport.com (Calls itself "The World's Longest-Running Climate Change Blog")
- www.coyoteblog.com/coyote_blog/2007/07/table-of-conten.html (Download a free copy of the book *A Skeptical Layman's Guide to Anthropogenic Global Warming*)
- http://epw.senate.gov/public/index.cfm?FuseAction=Minority.WelcomeMessage (Senator James Inhofe's website)
- http://techcentralstation.org (Not exclusively focused on global warming, but produces a lot of stuff on it and is well known)
- www.globalwarminghoax.com ("Refuting the Myth of Man-Made Global Warming" is its slogan)

WARMER SITES
These are useful sites with warmer resources not already mentioned in the text:

- http://gristmill.grist.org/skeptics (Comprehensive article on "How to Talk to a Climate Skeptic," offering rebuttals to most every common skeptical argument)
- www.realclimate.org (Run by climate scientists dedicated to communicating with the public)
- www.logicalscience.com (Gives its mission as "Defending the scientific consensus from vested interests")
- www.350.org (Global movement attempting to burn Humanity's Number into the collective consciousness; looks like they're having some wacky fun in the process, too)
- www.sourcewatch.org (Extensive and thorough site documenting the PR activities of sources; makes it extremely easy to figure out "How does this guy fit into the picture?" and it cites all of its statements)
- www.desmogblog.com (A comprehensive and up-to-date monitor of what's going on in the popular debate)
- http://wakeupfreakout.org ("Wake Up, Freak Out—Then Get a Grip" is an 11-minute animation that gives the most accessible explanation of abrupt climate change I've ever seen; I wish I had made it)

WIKIPEDIA ENTRIES GIVING AN OVERVIEW OF THE POPULAR DEBATE

Good overviews, and extremely useful to use as an index for where to look further:

- http://en.wikipedia.org/wiki/Global_warming_controversy
- http://en.wikipedia.org/wiki/Scientific_opinion_on_climate_change
- www.globalwarmingart.com/wiki/Statements_on_Climate_Change

NOTES

1 **Are you as sick:** Fingar, 2008.

1 **On the other:** Inhofe, 2003, 2007.

40 **Another way of stating:** Langenberg, 2008.

43 **Suppose I have:** Langenberg, 2008.

72 **And don't tell me:** Gilbert, 2006b.

72 **As an answer:** Gilbert, 2006a.

85 **A great example:** Coates and Henderson, 2007.

85 **However, when Durkin:** Conner, 2007.

90 **For instance, in 2006:** Billingsley, 2007.

91 **A few months later:** Lindzen, 2008.

105 **As economist Herman Daly:** Daly, 2007.

109 **In 2005, the NAS:** National Academy of Sciences, 2005.

110 **In 2006, AAAS:** American Association for the Advancement of Science, 2006.

110 **Abrupt climate changes of the magnitude:** National Academy Press, 2002.

111 **According to the chairman of the National Intelligence Council:** Fingar, 2008.

112 **Disruption and conflict:** Schwartz and Randall, 2003.

113 **The study calls:** Center for Naval Analyses, 2007b.

113 **Regarding arguments:** Center for Naval Analyses, 2007a.

113 **Another participant:** Center for Naval Analyses, 2007c.

114 **They found that:** Campbell et al., 2007.

115 **Perhaps the biggest:** U.S. Climate Action Partnership, 2007.

116 **The document emphasized a risk-management:** World Economic Forum and World Business Council for Sustainable Development, 2008.

118 **While Exxon hasn't signed:** Tillerson, 2007.

118 **And a January 2007:** Ball, 2007.

118 **In a speech in 2006:** Mufson and Eilperin, 2006.

118 **In the business-as-usual scenario:** Van der Veer, 2007.

119 **In 2008, the American Enterprise Institute:** Thernstrom, 2008.

120 **But a look at the process:** Intergovernmental Panel on Climate Change, 2007b.

120 **The 2007 report called:** Intergovernmental Panel on Climate Change, 2007a.

121 **A good illustration:** *New Zealand Herald*, 2008.

121 **Despite the existence:** An accessible description of what the IPCC is all about is available online at www.webcitation.org/5bWkvTx4w.

122 **The report concluded:** Stern, 2006.

123 **A total of 25 "senior economists":** Akerlof et al., 2005.

123 **Signed by more than 2,500 economists:** Arrow et al., 1997.

124 **In 2008:** Parry et al., 2008.

125 **His public statements:** Pilkington, 2008.

126 **In a peer-reviewed paper:** Hansen et al., 2008.

126 **A geologist and science historian:** Oreskes, 2004.

126 **In 2007, Oreskes:** Oreskes, 2007.

129 **As detailed on page 90:** Billingsley, 2007.

129 **The original statement said:** An excerpt of the 1999 statement is available online at www.globalwarmingart.com/wiki/Statements_on_Climate_Change.

129 **The new statement:** American Association of Petroleum Geologists, n.d.

130 **The Fraser Institute:** Fraser Institute, 2008.

131 **While the ISPM:** Fraser Institute, 2007.

132 **The Competitive Enterprise Institute:** The infamous ad is available online at www.youtube.com/watch?v=7sGKvDNdJNA.

133 **In my search:** Annett, 1998.

133 **According to the research:** Oreskes, 2007.

133 **While its online statement:** Marshall Institute, n.d.

133 **Written in 1999:** Boykoff, 2008.

134 **It states that:** Oregon Institute of Science and Medicine, n.d.

134 **First, it was promoted:** Malakoff, 1998.

135 **It's packaged as an official:** Inhofe, 2007.

135 **Signed by more than 500:** International Climate Science Coalition, 2008.

136 **In the introduction:** Science & Environmental Policy Project, 2007.

136 **When my initial research:** See "Leipzig Declaration" in Wikipedia at http://en.wikipedia.org/wiki/Leipzig_Declaration.

137 **Over the years:** Lindzen, 2001, 2006a, 2006b.

137 **Recently, his charges:** Lindzen, 2008.

138 **As far as the science:** Lindzen, 2006a.

139 **As far as expertise:** McKitrick, n.d.

139 **In 2007, he gave:** Carter, 2007.

140 **Based largely on:** Royte, 2001.

140 **Christy acknowledged:** Revkin, 2005.

140 **He believes the globe:** Spencer, 2008b.

141 **While McIntyre has:** McIntyre, 2005.

142 **"Simply put," he writes:** Lomborg, 2007, x.

145 **Writing a (non-peer-reviewed) paper:** Monckton, 2008.

146 **Inhofe's views and activities:** Inhofe, 2005.

160 **Imagine the planet's atmosphere:** I got this analogy from John Sterman, a professor at MIT, who was gracious enough to grant me permission to run with it. You simply *must* check out his online "simulator" based on the bathtub. You get to control emissions and see how they affect carbon levels. It may not look flashy, but it will blow your mind. While you're there, try out the Beer Game. Fascinating stuff. The URL is http://scripts .mit.edu/~jsterman/Management_Flight_Simulators_(MFS).html.

162 **It's now around 388:** Hansen et al., 2005.

164 **And you might get a sense:** Connor, 2006.

164 **A translation:** When translating geekspeak into bath-talk, pay close attention to whether a term is referring to *growth* of carbon emissions, carbon *emissions themselves,* or carbon *levels* in the atmosphere.

- Curbing (or slowing) the *growth* of emissions—the handle is still spinning open faster and faster, but it's not speeding up as quickly.
- Cutting the *growth* of emissions—the handle is still spinning open farther but at a constant speed.
- Stopping the *growth* of emissions—stopping the spinning of the handle. (The water is still flowing but now at a constant rate.)

- Cutting *emissions*—the handle is being cranked down, so that the water flows slower.
- Eliminating *emissions*—closing the handle entirely, shutting off the flow of water.
- Cutting carbon *levels* in the atmosphere—the drain is running faster than the spigot, and the water level in the tub is dropping.
- Carbon sequestration—the drain is being reamed out, so that water leaves the tub faster.

167 **In fact, 14,000 years ago:** Broecker, 2006.

167 **But this particular phenomenon:** National Snow and Ice Data Center, 2002.

171 **So here's the kicker:** Hansen et al., 2008.

174 **Researchers continued improving:** Steffensen et al., 2008.

174 **"It had to be captured":** Ohio State University, 2003.

175 **As climate researcher:** Pearce, 2006, xxv.

176 **So far, we've gone about:** Moore, 2008.

177 **Writing about the stunning:** Flückiger, 2008.

179 **And now come James Hansen:** Hansen et al., 2008.

184 **"Consensus as strong":** Kennedy, 2001.

186 **He's doing it because:** Romm, 2008.

187 **Probably the most surprising:** Because of time limits on YouTube, Bartlett's hour-long lecture has been broken up into eight segments. Here's the URL for the first one: www.youtube.com/watch?v=F-QA2rkpBSY. Once you're on the YouTube site, you'll find the links to the remaining segments. Even though the videos are of a lecture, with lots of graphs and delivered in a mild manner, every year when I show it to my students I invariably have a couple ask for their own copies! Now *that's* an endorsement.

191 **I share the view:** Schelling, 2007.

193 **One bombshell was the congressional:** *Arizona Republic*, 2008.

193 **And well-known economic:** Stein, 2008.

193 **It's pertinent to note:** Newman, 2008.

193 **"He always thinks through":** Newman, 2008.

194 **As the author Douglas Adams:** Adams and Carwardine, 1990, 174.

197 **The United States alone:** Ritholtz, 2008. Note also that the heads of state of 20 nations gathered for a weekend meeting in Washington, DC, on November 14–15, 2008, to discuss coordinated actions. Perhaps the

take-home lesson about the whole financial crisis for me can be summed up in a comment I overheard at a recent conference: "Okay, we've taken massive, immediate, coordinated action to save the financial system. So can we save the planet now, please?"

214 **Remember that he called:** Pilkington, 2008. Hansen's figure of 75 meters is so radically different from the IPCC's worst-case scenario because he is factoring in the possibility of the ice sheets melting, which was excluded from the IPCC models.

216 **Other peer-reviewed papers:** Anderson and Bows, 2008.

219 **It was this quote:** Hock, 1998.

222 **The scientist Richard Dawkins:** Dawkins, 1989.

230 **So if your hope:** Roosevelt, 1942.

REFERENCES

Adams, Douglas, and Mark Carwardine. 1990. *Last Chance to See*. Toronto: Stoddart.

Akerlof, George, et al. [Signatories]. 2005. "Statement by Leading Economists" [Petition]. Dec. 7. Available online at http://snurl.com/aj2ry.

American Association for the Advancement of Science. 2006. "AAAS Board Statement on Climate Change, Dec. 9. Available online at www.aaas .org/news/releases/2007/0218am_statement.shtml.

American Association of Petroleum Geologists, Division of Professional Affairs. n.d. "Position statement: Climate change." Available online at http://dpa.aapg.org/gac/statements/climatechange.cfm.

Analysis and Modelling Group. 2000. *An Assessment of the Economic and Environmental Implication for Canada of the Kyoto Protocol*. Natural Resources Canada.

Anderson, Kevin, and Alice Bows. 2008. "Reframing the Climate Change Challenge in Light of Post-2000 Emission Trends." *Philosophical Transactions of the Royal Society A*. Available online at www.tyndall.ac.uk/ publications/journal_papers/fulltext.pdf.

Annett, Alexander. 1998. *The Department of Energy's Report on the Impact of Kyoto: More Bad News for Americans*. Washington, DC: Heritage Foundation, Oct. 23. Available online at www.heritage.org/Research/ EnergyandEnvironment/BG1229.cfm.

"Arctic Melt Passes Tipping Point." 2008. *New Zealand Herald*, Dec. 22. Available online at http://snurl.com/agvrr.

Arrow, Kenneth, et al. [Signatories]. 1997. "Economists' Statement on Climate Change" [Petition]. Feb. 13. Available online at www.webcitation .org/5c3He2Wb7.

Ball, Jeffrey. 2007. "Exxon Mobil Softens Its Climate-Change Stance." *Wall Street Journal*, Jan. 11. Available online at http://snurl.com/74c5s.

Bartlett, Albert. n.d. "Arithmetic, Population, and Energy." Lecture at University of Colorado, Boulder. Available online under the title "The Most

Important Video You'll Ever See" at www.youtube.com/view_play_list?p=6A1FD147A45EF50D.

Billingsley, Lee. 2007. "Volunteers: Good for AAPG Climate." *AAPG Explorer*, Mar. Available online at www.aapg.org/explorer/president/2007/03mar.cfm.

Boykoff, Maxwell T. 2008. "Media and Scientific Communication: A Case of Climate Change." *Geological Society of London, Special Publications* 305: 11–18. Available online at www.eci.ox.ac.uk/publications/down loads/boykoff08-media-communication.pdf.

Broecker, Wallace S. 2006. "Was the Younger Dryas Triggered by a Flood?" *Science* 312 (5777): 1146–48. Available online at www.sciencemag.org/cgi/content/summary/312/5777/1146.

Brown, Lester. 2008. *Plan B 3.0: Mobilizing to Save Civilization*. New York: W. W. Norton.

Campbell, Kurt M., et al. 2007. "The Age of Consequences: The Foreign Policy and National Security Implications of Global Climate Change." Washington, DC: CSIS and CNAS. Available online at http://snurl.com/7lpwx.

Carter, Robert M. 2007. "Testing the Hypothesis of Dangerous Human-Caused Global Warming." Paper given at the Climate Conference [Heartland Institute], New York, Mar. 2.

Center for Naval Analyses. 2007a. "Climate Change Poses Serious Threat to U.S. National Security" [Press Release]. Apr. 16. Available online at http://securityandclimate.cna.org/news/releases/070416.aspx.

Center for Naval Analyses. 2007b. "National Security and the Threat of Climate Change." Virginia. Available online at http://snurl.com/7lnvw.

Center for Naval Analyses. 2007c. "National Security and the Threat of Climate Change" [Power Point presentation]. Available online at http://securityandclimate.cna.org/report/CNA_NatlSecurityAndThe ThreatOfClimateChange.pdf.

Coates, Sam, and Mark Henderson. 2007. C4's "Debate on Global Warming Boils Over." *TimesOnline* (UK), Mar. 15. Available online at http://snurl.com/73ydr.

Committee on Abrupt Climate Change et al. 2002. *Abrupt Climate Change: Inevitable Surprises*. Washington, DC: National Academy Press. Available online at www.nap.edu/catalog.php?record_id=10136#description.

Connor, Steve. 2006. "Global Growth in Carbon Emissions Is 'Out of Control.'" *The Independent* (UK), Nov. 11. Available online at www .independent.co.uk/environment/climate-change/global-growth-in -carbon-emissions-is-out-of-control-423822.html.

Connor, Steve. 2007. "C4 Accused of Falsifying Data in Documentary on Climate Change." *The Independent* (UK), May 8. Available online at http://snurl.com/73ycd.

Crichton, Michael. 2004. *State of Fear*. New York: Avon.

Daly, Herman. 2007. Keynote Address: "Federal Climate Policy: Design Principles and Remaining Needs" workshop, American Meteorological Society. Washington, DC, Nov. 13. Available online at www.climatepolicy .org/?p=65.

Dawkins, Richard. 1989. *The Selfish Gene*. Oxford: Oxford University Press.

Energy Information Agency. 1998. *Impacts of the Kyoto Protocol on U.S. Energy Markets and Economic Activity*. Washington, DC: U.S. Department of Energy. Available online at http://tonto.eia.doe.gov/ftproot/service/ oiaf9803.pdf.

Essex, Christopher, and Ross McKitrick. 2008. *Taken by Storm: The Troubled Science, Policy, and Politics of Global Warming*. Toronto: Key Porter Books.

Fingar, Thomas. House Permanent Select Committee on Intelligence, House Select Committee on Energy Independence and Global Warming. 2008. *National Intelligence Assessment on the National Security Implications of Global Climate Change to 2030, Statement for the Record*. June 25. Available online at www.dni.gov/testimonies/20080625_ testimony.pdf

Flückiger, Jacqueline. 2008. "Did You Say 'Fast'?" *Science* 321 (5889): 650–51. Available online at www.scienceonline.org/cgi/content/ short/321/5889/650.

Fraser Institute. 2007. "Independent Summary Shows New UN Climate Change Report Refutes Alarmism and Reveals Major Uncertainties in the Science" [News Release]. Feb. 5. Available online at www .fraserinstitute.org/newsandevents/news/4163.aspx.

Fraser Institute. 2008. "What We Think." Available online at www .fraserinstitute.org/aboutus/whatwethink.htm.

Gilbert, Daniel. 2006a. "If Only Gay Sex Caused Global Warming," *LA Times*, July 2. Available online at http://snurl.com/73yfd.

Gilbert, Daniel. 2006b. "It's the End of the World as We Know It" [Blog Post]. Available online at http://snurl.com/73yh8.

Hansen, James, et al. 2005. "Earth's Energy Imbalance: Confirmation and Implications." *Science* 308 (5727): 1431–35. Available online at www.sciencemag.org/cgi/content/abstract/308/5727/1431.

Hansen, James, et al. 2008. "Target Atmospheric CO_2: Where Should Humanity Aim?" *Open Atmospheric Science Journal* 2: 217–31. Available online at http://arxiv.org/pdf/0804.1126v3.

Hock, Dee W. 1998. "The Birth of the Chaordic Century: Out of Control and Into Order." Available online at www.webcitation.org/5e16bTjvh.

"A Humbled Sage" [Opinion]. 2008, *Arizona Republic*, Oct. 28. Available online at www.azcentral.com/arizonarepublic/opinions/articles/2008/10/28/20081028tue2-28.html.

Inhofe, James. 2003. "The Science of Climate Change" [U.S. Senate Floor Statement], July 28. Available online at http://inhofe.senate.gov/pressreleases/climate.htm.

Inhofe, James. 2005. "Climate Change Update" [U.S. Senate Floor Statement], Jan 4. Available online at http://inhofe.senate.gov/pressreleases/climateupdate.htm.

Inhofe, James, Office of. 2007. *U.S. Senate Report: Over 400 Prominent Scientists Disputed Man-Made Global Warming Claims in 2007* [Minority Staff Report]. Available online at http://epw.senate.gov/public/index.cfm?FuseAction=Files.View&FileStore_id=bba2ebce-6d03-48e4-b83c-44fe321a34fa.

Intergovernmental Panel on Climate Change. 2007a. *Climate Change 2007: Synthesis Report: Summary for Policymakers.* Available online at www.ipcc.ch/pdf/assessment-report/ar4/syr/ar4_syr_spm.pdf.

Intergovernmental Panel on Climate Change. 2007b. "The IPCC 4th Assessment Report Is Coming Out" [Flyer]. Available online at www.ipcc.ch/pdf/press-ar4/ipcc-flyer-low.pdf.

International Climate Science Coalition. 2008. "The Manahattan Declaration on Climate Change." Presented at the International Conference on Climate Change, New York, Mar. 4. Available online at www.climatescienceinternational.org/index.php?option=com_content&task=view&id=37&Itemid=54.

Kennedy, Donald. 2001. "An Unfortunate U-Turn on Carbon." *Science* 29 (5513): 2515.

Langenberg, Donald. 2008. Private communication [email], Aug. 22.

Lindzen, Richard. 2001. "The Press Gets It Wrong: Our Report Doesn't Support the Kyoto Treaty" [Opinion]. *Wall Street Journal*, June 11. Available online at www.opinionjournal.com/editorial/feature.html?id=95000606.

Lindzen, Richard. 2006a. "Climate of Fear: Global-Warming Alarmists Intimidate Dissenting Scientists into Silence" [Opinion]. *Wall Street Journal*, Apr. 12. Available online at www.opinionjournal.com/extra/?id=110008220.

Lindzen, Richard. 2006b. "Don't Believe the Hype: Al Gore Is Wrong. There's No 'Consensus' on Global Warming" [Opinion]. *Wall Street Journal*, July 2. Available online at www.opinionjournal.com/extra/?id=110008597.

Lindzen, Richard. 2008. "Climate Science: Is It Currently Designed to Answer Questions?" Paper presented to the Creativity and Creative Inspiration in Mathematics, Science, and Engineering: Developing a Vision for the Future meetings, San Marino, Aug. 29–31. Available online at http://arxiv.org/pdf/0809.3762v3.

Lomborg, Bjorn. 2001. *The Skeptical Environmentalist: Measuring the Real State of the World*. Cambridge: Cambridge University Press.

Lomborg, Bjorn. 2007. *Cool It: The Skeptical Environmentalist's Guide to Global Warming*. New York: Knopf.

Malakoff, David. 1998. "Advocacy Mailing Draws Fire." *Science* 280 (5361): 195. Available online at www.sciencemag.org/cgi/content/summary/280/5361/195a.

Marshall Institute. n.d. "Climate Change." Available online at www.marshall.org/subcategory.php?id=9.

McIntyre, Steve. 2005. FAQ 2005. Available online at www.climateaudit.org/?page_id=1002.

McKitrick, Ross. n.d. "Global Warming: Competing Views." Available online at www.uoguelph.ca/~rmckitri/cc.html.

Monckton, Christopher. 2008. "Climate Sensitivity Reconsidered." *Physics & Society* 37 (3): 6–9. Available online at www.aps.org/units/fps/newsletters/200807/upload/july08.pdf.

Moore, Frances C. 2008. "Carbon Dioxide Emissions Accelerating Rapidly." Earth Policy Institute, Apr. 9. Available online at www.earth-policy.org/Indicators/CO2/2008.htm.

Mufson, Steven, and Juliet Eilperin. 2006. "Energy Firms Come to Terms with Climate Change." *Washington Post*, Nov. 25. Available online at http://snurl.com/7lu4w.

National Academy of Sciences. 2005. "Joint Science Academies' Statement: Global Response to Climate Change." Available online at www.nationalacademies.org/onpi/06072005.pdf.

National Snow and Ice Data Center. 2002. "Larsen B Ice Shelf Collapses in Antarctica." Press Room [Press Release]. Mar. 18. Available online at http://nsidc.org/news/press/larsen_B/2002.html.

Newman, Rick. 2008. "Greenspan vs. Buffett." *U.S. News & World Report*, Oct. 27. Available online at www.usnews.com/blogs/flowchart/2008/10/27/greenspan-vs-buffett.html.

Ohio State University. 2003. "Ice Cores May Yield Clues to 5,000-Year-Old Mystery." *ScienceDaily*, Nov. 7. Available online at www.sciencedaily.com/releases/2003/11/031107055850.htm.

Oregon Institute of Science and Medicine. n.d. Global Warming Petition Project. Available online at www.petitionproject.org.

Oreskes, Naomi. 2004. "Beyond the Ivory Tower: The Scientific Consensus on Climate Change." *Science* 306 (5702): 1686. Available online at www.sciencemag.org/cgi/content/full/306/5702/1686.

Oreskes, Naomi. 2007. "The Truth About Denial" [Jeffrey B. Graham Lecture Series]. Paper presented at the Scripps Institution of Oceanography, La Jolla, Calif., Oct. 8. Available online at www.youtube.com/watch?v=2T4UF_Rmlio.

Parry, M. L., et al. 2008. "U.S. Scientists and Economists' Call for Swift and Deep Cuts in Greenhouse Gas Emissions," May. Available online at www.ucsusa.org/climateletter.

Pearce, Fred. 2006. *With Speed and Violence: Why Scientists Fear Tipping Points in Climate Change*. Boston: Beacon.

Pilkington, Ed. 2008. "Climate Target Is Not Radical Enough." *The Guardian*, Apr. 7. Available online at www.guardian.co.uk/environment/2008/apr/07/climatechange.carbonemissions.

Revkin, Andy. 2005. "Errors Cited in Assessing Climate Data." *New York Times*, Aug. 12. Available online at www.nytimes.com/2005/08/12/science/earth/12climate.long.html.

Ritholtz, Barry. 2008. "Big Bailouts, Bigger Bucks" [Blog Post]. Available online at www.ritholtz.com/blog/2008/11/big-bailouts-bigger-bucks.

Romm, Joseph. 2008. "Ain't No Wind in T. Boone Pickens' Sails." *Salon*, Aug.

28. Available online at www.salon.com/env/feature/2008/08/28/t_boone_pickens/index.html.

Roosevelt, Franklin D. 1942. State of the Union Address to Congress. Jan. 6.

Royte, Elizabeth. 2001. "The Gospel According to John." *Discover*, Feb. 1. Available online at http://discovermagazine.com/2001/feb/featgospel.

Schelling, Thomas C. 2007. "Climate Change: The Uncertainties, the Certainties and What They Imply About Action." *The Economists' Voice* 4: 3. Available online at www.bepress.com/ev/vol4/iss3/art3.

Schwartz, Peter, and Doug Randall. 2003. *An Abrupt Climate Change Scenario and Its Implications for United States National Security*. Washington, DC: Pentagon. Available online at www.grist.org/pdf/AbruptClimateChange2003.pdf.

Science & Environmental Policy Project. 2007. "Preface: NIPCC vs. IPCC." *The Week That Was*, Sept. 1. Available online at www.sepp.org/Archive/weekwas/2007/September%201.htm.

Singer, Fred S., and Dennis T. Avery. 2008. *Unstoppable Global Warming: Every 1,500 Years*. Lanham, MD: Rowman & Littlefield.

Spencer, Roy. 2008a. *Climate Confusion: How Global Warming Hysteria Leads to Bad Science, Pandering Politicians and Misguided Policies That Hurt the Poor*. New York: Encounter Books.

Spencer, Roy W. 2008b. Testimony before the Senate Environment and Public Works Committee, July 22. Available online at www.webcitation.org/5cu7hl2KM.

Steffensen, Jorgen Peder, et al. 2008. "High-Resolution Greenland Ice Core Data Show Abrupt Climate Change Happens in Few Years." *Science* 321 (5889): 680–84. Available online at www.sciencemag.org/cgi/content/Fabstract/321/5889/680.

Stein, Ben. 2008. "You Don't Always Know When the Sky Will Fall." *New York Times*, Oct. 28. Available online at www.nytimes.com/2008/10/26/business/26every.html.

Stern, Nicholas. 2006. "Stern Review on the Economics of Climate Change" [Executive Summary]. London: HM Treasury. Available online at www.hm-treasury.gov.uk/d/Executive_Summary.pdf.

Thernstrom, Samuel. 2008. "Resetting Earth's Thermostat." *On the Issues*, June 27. Available online at www.aei.org/publications/pubID.28202/pub_detail.asp.

Tillerson, Rex. 2007. "Rex Tillerson: CERAWeek" [Opening Address]. *BusinessWeek*, Feb. 13. Available online at http://snurl.com/749ex.

U.S. Climate Action Partnership. 2007. *A Call for Action*. Washington, DC. Available online at www.us-cap.org/USCAPCallForAction.pdf.

Van der Veer, Jeroen. 2007. "Two Energy Futures." *Project Syndicate*. Available online at www.project-syndicate.org/commentary/vanderveer1.

World Economic Forum and World Business Council for Sustainable Development. 2008. *CEO Climate Policy Recommendations to G8 Leaders*. Geneva, Switzerland: World Economic Forum. Available online at www.weforum.org/documents/initiatives/CEOStatement.pdf.

ACKNOWLEDGMENTS

I am nothing if not a voracious asker of questions. So many people indulged me during this project that at times I didn't feel so much an author as I did a representative, a funnel for the collective experience and wisdom of others. I am grateful for all that they gave me, in so many forms. All of their contributions, great or small, have formed this book.

Thank you to Professor Richard Gammon of the University of Washington, for showing me how the pieces all fit together in that one lecture, years ago.

I want to thank Richard Lindzen, Steve McIntyre, Ross McKitrick, James Hansen, Bill McKibben, Joe Romm, Naomi Oreskes, Donald Langenberg, Ross Gelbspan, Carl Bergstrom, Gavin Schmidt, Roger Pielke Jr., Mark Lynas, Robert May, Terry Goodkind, Richard Muller, Patrick Moore, John Sterman, Richard Feely, and Mary Wood, for taking the time from their schedules to provide a critique of my ideas or to answer my questions, from the mundane to the intractable. Any errors that remain are mine. These are very busy people, and the fact that they responded to Just Another Guy on the Internet speaks to their generosity and dedication.

I especially appreciated the extensive conversations that Roger Pielke Sr., Don Langenberg, Spencer Weart, and Dimitri Zenghelis granted me. They were invaluable.

I want to acknowledge the role that all my students played over the years in helping me sharpen and clarify my thinking by lending me their brains every day as we tackle knotty questions.

My agent at Paradigm, Jason Yarn, and my editors at Perigee Books, Meg Leder and Maria Gagliano, showed remarkable patience in taking this thrashing, obsessive amateur and trying to get a professional book out of him—no easy task, and I thank them for it.

This book relied heavily on the selfless help offered by the online community at www.manpollo.org, as well as some of their friends who were pulled in. They volunteered their time to serve as a sort of online think tank and researcher pool for me when I needed to refine an idea or find some piece of information. You all have inspired me and give me hope. Thank you for that.

I have gotten help from so many people during the course of this project that I am sure I neglected some names, for which I apologize. Your contributions live in this book, and I thank you.

But the greatest credit goes to my wife, whose heroic tolerance made this book possible. She has effectively been a single mother since I posted the first video over a year and a half ago. We had no idea what we were in for, and she has endured it with a patience and selflessness that is nothing less than remarkable. No one else in the world would have tolerated me as I put her through hell with my obsession with getting this simple little grid out to the world. Thank you so much. I'm done now, sweetheart.

And they won't understand this now, but they will when they read this in the future: thank you, Katie and Alex. Thank you for the moments of joy that replenished me. And thank you for what I took from you without asking: The time we didn't share together. I am so sorry I wasn't there for you more during such an influential time in your lives. It was an anguishing choice that I made every day, but I hope that you will understand that I took that time away from you in an attempt to give you something even more fundamental—your security. It may not be enough, but I did all that I could.

INDEX

Page numbers in *italics* represent illustrations.

ABOUT THE AUTHOR

Photo by Ari Denison

Greg Craven grew up on a farm in Oregon, experimented with different jobs for a decade, and finally found his calling as a high school physics and chemistry teacher. His main qualification for proposing a layman's approach to climate change is having borrowed the 30 brains in his classroom every period to mull questions of science and critical thinking for the last 10 years. He's found there's no better way to refine a thought than to toss it out in front of a roomful of critical teenagers. He is a bit surprised to find he's written a book as a result. Craven lives in Corvallis, Oregon, with his wife and two young daughters.